# Credits

**National Geographic's
Driving Guides To America
The Rockies**

*By* THOMAS SCHMIDT
*Photographed by* MICHAEL LEWIS

**Published by**
THE NATIONAL GEOGRAPHIC SOCIETY

Reg Murphy
*President and Chief Executive Officer*
Gilbert M. Grosvenor
*Chairman of the Board*
Nina D. Hoffman
*Senior Vice President*

**Prepared by The Book Division**

William R. Gray
*Vice President and Director*
Charles Kogod
*Assistant Director*
Barbara A. Payne
*Editorial Director*

**Driving Guides to America**

Elizabeth L. Newhouse
*Director of Travel Books
and Series Editor*
Cinda Rose
*Art Director*
Thomas B. Powell III
*Illustrations Editor*
Caroline Hickey, Barbara A. Noe
*Senior Researchers*
Carl Mehler
*Map Editor and Designer*

**Staff for this book**

Elizabeth L. Newhouse
*Editor*
Cinda Rose
*Art Director*
Thomas B. Powell III
*Illustrations Editor*

Caroline Hickey
*Chief Researcher*
Carl Mehler
*Map Editor and Designer*

Mary Luders
*Assistant Editor*
Carol Bittig Lutyk
*Contributing Editor*

Thomas L. Gray, Joseph Ochlak
*Map Researchers*
Martin S. Walz, James Huckenpahler
*Map Production*
Tibor G. Tóth
*Map Relief*

Gwen Shaffer
*Researcher*
Meredith Wilcox
*Illustrations Assistant*

Richard S. Wain
*Production Project Manager*
Lewis R. Bassford, Lyle Rosbotham
*Production*

Kevin G. Craig, Dale M. Herring,
Joshua S. Lazarus, Peggy J. Oxford,
Jennifer A. Serrano
*Staff Assistants*

Anne Marie Houppert
*Indexer*

Jennifer Emmett, Michael H. Higgins,
Mary E. Jennings, Sandra F. Lotterman,
Dean Nadalin
*Contributors*

**Manufacturing
and Quality Management**

George V. White, *Director*
John T. Dunn, *Associate Director*
Vincent P. Ryan, *Manager*

Cover: Maroon Bells, Colorado
PAUL CHESLEY

Previous pages: Many Glacier Area,
Glacier National Park, Montana

Facing page: Appaloosa Museum,
Moscow, Idaho

4

Rocky Mountain wildflowers

Top of Rendezvous Mountain, Jackson Hole, Wyoming

National Geographic's
Driving Guides to America

# The Rockies

By Thomas Schmidt
Photographed by Michael Lewis

Prepared by
The Book Division
National Geographic Society
Washington, D.C.

# Contents

Cedar grove, Ross Creek, Montana

8

## More than Mountains

It would be wrong to think of the Rockies strictly in terms of mountains. Between the ranges lie semiarid valleys thick with sagebrush. There are shortgrass prairies, wide deserts, fields of sand dunes, lava plains, volcanic cones, deep river gorges, buttes, and mesas. Major rivers gather and flow east or west, and the Great Plains spill away from the mountains' bases.

In the Rockies you'll find five major national parks and dozens of national monuments, wildlife refuges, and historical sites that preserve spectacular ecosystems, ancient Indian settlements, frontier outposts, rich fossil beds, and battlefields. And people have roamed the area for more than 11,000 years.

When I was 14, I lived for a summer in an abandoned gold-mining camp high in Montana's Ruby Range. It was just a string of cabins in the woods, with a tiny creek out back for water and a pair of old Montanans for neighbors—Frank and Virginia, the caretakers. They knew how to pan for gold, shoot plumb, wrangle cows, change out engines, and build what they needed. They worked hard, owned little, but regarded themselves as richer than most.

"Aw, Bus," she'd say to Frank, putting her arms around him. "Look at it, will ya? Just *look* at it."

"It" might have been a glimmering smear of stars across the night sky or a glassy mountain lake reflecting the cliffs at sunset. Whatever it was, she'd seen it hundreds of times before, and yet it still held the power to swell and refresh her soul. So it goes in the Rockies, a land of such compelling beauty, such variety, such intricacy and surprises, that even one small valley can snag your heart for a lifetime.

This book takes in more than 1,000 miles of the Rocky Mountain range—the mountains of Idaho, Montana, Wyoming, and Colorado—and a vast and varied landscape.

If you're planning a trip to the Rockies, you might keep a few things in mind. First, forget spring. It's wet, it's cold, it's overcast, and in the mountains it can linger into June. Spring is when locals do one of two things: mope or bug out for the Southwest. Unless you're a skier or snowmobiler, the best times to visit are summer and autumn. Remember that the seasons vary with elevation, and mountain weather is unpredictable. Also, distances are deceptive. Some roads seem dangerous at 35 miles per hour. And if the curves don't slow you down, the scenery, or a museum, or a historical site probably will. So be prepared for some pleasant delays, and expect to echo my friend Virginia's words:

"Look at it, will ya? Just *look* at it."

**THOMAS SCHMIDT**

# About the Guides

*N*ATIONAL GEOGRAPHIC'S DRIVING GUIDES TO AMERICA invite you on memorable road trips through the United States and Canada. Intended both as travel planners and companions, each volume guides you on preplanned tours over a wide variety of terrain to the best places to see and things to do. The authors, expert regional travel writers, star-rate (from none to two ★★) the drives and points of interest to make sure you don't miss their favorites.

All distances and drive times are approximate (if you linger, as you should, plan on considerably more time). Recommended seasons are the best times to go, but roads and sites are open all year unless otherwise noted. Besides the stated days of operation, many sites close on national holidays. For the most up-to-date site information, it's best to call ahead when possible.

Then, with this book and a road map, set off on your adventure through this awesomely beautiful land.

Going-to-the-Sun Road,
Glacier National Park, Montana

## MAP KEY and ABBREVIATIONS

| | | |
|---|---|---|
| Memorial Parkway (National) | | Featured Drive |
| National Monument | NAT. MON. | |
| National Park | N.P. | Interstate Highway |
| National Recreation Area | NAT. REC. AREA, N.R.A. | (94) |
| National Reserve | NAT. RESERVE | |
| | | U.S. Federal Highway |
| National Forest | NAT. FOR., N.F. | (12) |
| National Grassland | NAT. GRASSLAND | |
| Wilderness (National) | | State Road |
| | | (29) |
| U.S. Fish and Wildlife Service | | |
| National Bison Range | NAT. BISON RANGE | County, Local, or Provincial Road |
| National Elk Refuge | | [A] |
| National Wildlife Refuge | N.W.R. | |
| Bureau of Land Management | | |
| National Conservation Area | N.C.A. | Historical Trail |
| Primitive Area | | |
| | | |
| Mountain Park | | Railroad |
| State Park | S.P. | |
| State Recreation Area | S.R.A. | |
| | | State or National Border |
| Indian Reservation | I.R. | |

Forest / Wilderness Boundary

### ADDITIONAL ABBREVIATIONS

| | |
|---|---|
| A.F.B. | *Air Force Base* |
| Cr. | *Creek* |
| HWY. | *Highway* |
| Mt.-s | *Mountain-s* |
| N. Fk. | *North Fork* |
| N.H.P. | *National Historical Park* |
| N.H.S. | *National Historic Site* |
| REC. AREA | *Recreation Area* |
| Res. | *Reservoir* |
| S. Fk. | *South Fork* |
| SPR. | *Spring* |
| S.H.S. | *State Historic Site* |

■    Point of Interest

★    State Capital

|    Dam

=    Falls

)(    Pass

# Bozeman to Yellowstone

**350 miles ● 3 days ● Mid-June through mid-Oct. ● Most roads in Yellowstone National Park close from Nov. to May. Information: 307-344-7381**

See p. 32

See p. 20

See p. 90

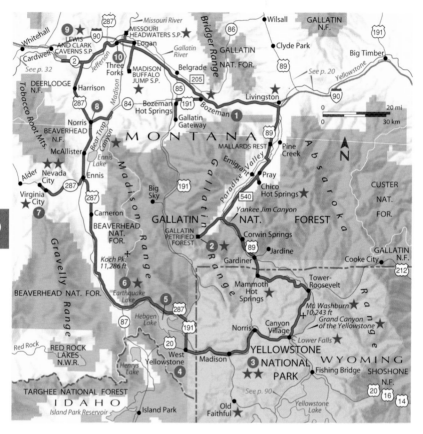

Looping through the heart of Yellowstone National Park, this magnificent drive follows some of the West's most famous trout-fishing rivers through spectacular country—winding chasms, deep forests, dazzling wild-flower meadows, and spacious sagebrush valleys sprawling at the foot of dramatic mountain ranges. The route also has its share of museums, historic sites, and such pleasant diversions as hot springs pools and strange music machines designed to entertain boozy miners.

The route starts in Bozeman with a visit to one of Montana's finest museums, then curves around the base of the Gallatin and Bridger Ranges to Livingston, where it picks up the Yellowstone River and heads south through

Paradise Valley to the park. Within the park, it takes in geyser basins, hot springs, and several thundering waterfalls, and offers opportunities to see elk, pronghorn, deer, moose, and—possibly—grizzly bears. Exiting the park, the drive follows the Madison River through the site of a major earthquake, then turns north to Ennis, where there's a side trip to the 1860s mining towns of Virginia City and Nevada City. It ends in the Three Forks area, where you can tour Lewis and Clark Caverns and view the headwaters of the Missouri River.

John Bozeman's famous cutoff from the Oregon Trail to the Montana gold fields led through the expansive valley where ❶ **Bozeman** ★ *(Chamber of Commerce 406-586-5421)* now stands amid three mountain ranges. Several historic districts reflect the prosperity that came with the arrival of the railroad and university in the 1880s and '90s. Enjoy Bozeman's vigorous downtown area, then wander past Victorian houses in the **South Willson Historic District.** The old neighborhood leads to the university campus and the **Museum of the Rockies** ★★ *(600 W. Kagy Blvd. 406-994-2251. Adm. fee),* noted for its planetarium, dinosaur exhibits, Native American artifact displays, and lovingly restored buggies, wagons, early autos, and other frontier relics. Perhaps the most interesting exhibit interprets the geology and evolution of life in the region. Outdoors, visit the Tinsley Homestead *(summer only)* and its 1889 log house.

Outside town, along US 191, soak at **Bozeman Hot Springs** *(8 miles W. 406-587-3030. Adm. fee)* and dawdle at the 1927 **Gallatin Gateway Inn** *(14 miles SW. 406-763-4672),* an elegant railway hotel built on a major route into Yellowstone.

From **Livingston** ★ (see Custer Country drive, p. 20), head south on US 89 through **Paradise Valley**—a roomy place of grass and rumpled hills between the Gallatin and Absaroka (ab-SORE-kuh) Ranges. It's a dreamy stretch of road, with

Voss Inn, South Willson Historic District, Bozeman

a world-class trout-fishing river, the Yellowstone, sweeping along the foot of the grand Absarokas. About 12 miles south of town, dip your toes and watch the boats glide

# Bozeman to Yellowstone

Rockies' bison

### Early Autos in the Park

Considering the long columns of cars, trucks, and RVs that traverse Yellowstone's roads today, it may be difficult to imagine the park without automobiles. And yet cars were banned from the park at the turn of the century because they scared teams of horses and they threatened the upper-class tourism monopoly enjoyed by the park's concessionaires. When finally autos were allowed to enter the park, beginning in 1915, the speed limit was 12 mph going uphill, 10 coming down, 8 when approaching sharp curves, and never more than 20 mph. You were clocked from one station to the next, and if you arrived too soon, you got a speeding ticket.

past **Mallards Rest** fishing access site, a shady bench of sand and gravel with views of the glaciated Absaroka-Beartooth high country.

About 5 miles south of Mallards Rest, cross the Yellowstone River and pick up Route 540, which offers good views of the Gallatin Range and avoids the rush of traffic on US 89. From Pray take the turnoff to **Chico Hot Springs** ★ *(406-333-493. Adm. fee),* one of Montana's best commercial soaking pools set in a rustic 1900 lodge with a famous saloon and excellent restaurant to boot.

Soon, the road rejoins US 89. High in the hills to the west lies the ❷ **Gallatin Petrified Forest** ★ *(Follow Tom Miner Rd. to trailhead. 406-848-7375),* where a half-mile interpretive trail leads through the petrified remains of forests that grew here 35 to 55 million years ago. You can take home a small sample, but first pick up a free permit at the Gallatin National Forest office in Livingston *(5242 US 89S).*

Follow the Yellowstone through **Yankee Jim Canyon,** a narrow gorge cut through Precambrian metamorphic rock. Twice a year, the largest wildlife migration in the lower 48 states takes place along the river between the canyon and Gardiner. Thousands of elk, deer, pronghorn, bighorn sheep, and bison graze the slopes as they travel between the park and their winter feeding grounds.

From Gardiner, enter ❸ **Yellowstone National Park** ★ ★ *(Headquarters 307-344-7381. Adm. fee)* through the **Theodore Roosevelt Entrance Arch,** built in 1903 and dedicated by Roosevelt himself. Best known for its steaming geysers, hot springs, fumaroles, and other geothermal curiosities, the park takes in an immense, though relatively gentle terrain of vast rolling forests interrupted by broad meadows and spacious valleys teeming with bison, elk, moose, and deer. Its web of achingly beautiful rivers and creeks stream out in all directions—thundering over waterfalls, cutting deep canyons and intimate gorges, filling large lakes, and meandering across open grassy flats.

This serene sanctuary for wolves, bears, bighorn sheep, and trumpeter swans belies a violent geologic past. Three times in the last 2 million years (most recently 600,000 years ago), volcanic explosions rocked Yellowstone—literally blowing off its lid. The latest explosion resulted in the collapse of the central portion of the park and the formation of a basin, or caldera, 28 by 47 miles.

In **Mammoth Hot Springs** ★ drop by the **Albright Visitor Center** ★, housed in one of several stone buildings erected in 1909 as Army officers' quarters. Exhibits depict the lives of Yellowstone's soldiers, who administered the park from 1886, as well as the lives of early park rangers, who took over in 1916. Here, too, hang some treasures: watercolor sketches of geyser basins and waterfalls by Thomas Moran and early photographs by William Henry Jackson.

Nearby, poke your head into the **Mammoth Hot Springs Hotel** *(307-344-7311)* lobby, built in the '30s, then head for Mammoth Hot Springs proper—the creamy brow

13

Sunrise on the Madison River, Yellowstone National Park

of steaming rock beyond the buildings. **Upper Terrace Drive** curves among the large travertine terraces and mounds and passes dead limber pines more than 500 years old. For a close-up look at active springs trickling over stair-stepping terraces, follow the nature trail through the **Main Terrace** area, where hot water deposits some of the two tons of travertine accumulated here daily.

Double back to the hotel and turn right on the **Tower-Roosevelt** road, part of the Grand Loop Road. Soon you'll

Stagecoach at the Mammoth Hot Springs Hotel, Yellowstone National Park

14

come to **Undine Falls,** a lovely twin falls that drops 60 feet, then 50 feet through a narrow gorge.

Even if you're not caught in an endless column of RVs, get off the main drag and follow **Blacktail Plateau Drive** through rolling sagebrush hills and evergreen forests— good country for spotting pronghorn, elk, and deer. Shortly after rejoining the main road, take the right-hand turnoff for **Petrified Tree,** one of many redwoods in the region buried alive by volcanic ash 50 million years ago and turned to stone.

Rustic **Roosevelt Lodge** *(307-344-7311)* was built in 1920 and named for Teddy Roosevelt, who camped near here during his 1903 junket to dedicate his namesake entrance arch. Near the ranger station, have a look at the **Tower Soldier Station,** one of three such Army outposts that survive. On the way to Canyon Village, stop to stretch your legs at **Tower Fall ★,** where a short trail leads to an overlook above a 132-foot cascade spilling from a cluster of coarse volcanic towers.

Beyond the falls, the road climbs above a broad valley drained by Antelope Creek—prime grizzly habitat and one of the best roadside locations in the park to spot the great bears. After scoping the valley for grizzlies, drive to the **Mount Washburn ★** parking area and consider a walk to the top of this extinct volcano. The moderate 3-mile hike leads through spectacular subalpine meadows where bighorn sheep often munch on wildflowers. It ends at a fire lookout with a 50- to 100-mile panoramic view.

As the road continues its climb toward Dunraven Pass, it's hard to miss the effects of the great Wolf Lake Fire that burned through here in 1988. Many of the large mammals that died during that amazing season were killed among the cliffs of this rugged area, trapped by the swift fires.

A few miles beyond the pass, stop at the **Washburn Hot Springs Overlook** for a view of the **Grand Canyon of the Yellowstone** ★—a ragged trench cut through the forests of central Yellowstone. Here, too, you get a feel for the immense size of the Yellowstone Caldera, which stretches south 35 miles from the slopes of Mount Washburn to the Red Mountains.

Minerva Terrace, Mammoth Hot Springs

At **Canyon Village** follow the **North Rim Road** ★ along the edge of the canyon to **Inspiration Point** ★. The canyon, with its vivid smears of color, measures 1,200 feet at its deepest and up to 4,000 feet across and 20 miles long. Stop at **Grandview Point** to see the canyon's breadth and at **Lookout Point** for the classic north rim view of 308-foot **Lower Falls** ★—a grand, thundering column of foam, one of the most impressive cascades in the Rockies. Another spur road leads to the brink of **Upper Falls** ★, which drops 109 feet. A short walk from the parking area leads to yet another cascade: 129-foot **Crystal Falls.** A third spur road, to **Artist Point** ★, leads over Chittenden

15

Norris Geyser Basin, Yellowstone National Park

Bridge and hugs the south rim. Trails here lead to close-up views of both falls, and Artist Point offers perhaps the most famous vista of the canyon and Lower Falls.

Double back to Canyon Village and take the road to Norris. Along the way, a 3-mile side road follows the Gibbon River to **Virginia Cascade,** which tumbles 60 feet down cliffs. Look for moose in the willow grove above the falls.

**Norris Geyser Basin ★** may be the hottest cluster of geysers in the park and the most active. For a lesson on geothermal plumbing and an educated guess on when the next geyser may erupt, drop by the sturdy **Norris Museum ★**—a 1930s log-and-stone classic built by the Civilian Conservation Corps. Nearby, the **Back Basin Nature Trail,** a 1.5-mile loop, passes the highest active geyser in the world, 380-foot **Steamboat Geyser.**

From Norris, head southwest toward Madison. You'll pass more springs, geysers, and paint pots as you approach **Gibbon Falls,** which pours over the rim of the Yellowstone Caldera and drops 84 feet. At Madison you're just 16 miles from the geysers and hot springs of the **Old Faithful ★** area, so a side trip may be in order.

The main route continues west along the **Madison River,** one of the world's great trout streams, which flows between lava walls 1,000 feet high. Bison stump along the forested banks, elk graze riverside meadows, and snow-white trumpeter swans glide across the water. All too soon, the road leaves the park at the west exit.

A town of motels, T-shirt shops, and rubber tomahawk outlets, ❹ **West Yellowstone** *(Chamber of Commerce 406-646-7701)* may be the curio capital of Montana, but it's also a very serious, highly sophisticated fly-fishing center. Even if you don't fish, the tackle shops are worth a visit to gawk at the pricey gadgetry and bins of hand-tied flies.

For a close look at grizzly bears and gray wolves in a first-rate zoo setting, stop by the **Grizzly Discovery Center** *(Near park entrance. 406-646-7001 or 800-257-2570. Adm. fee),* where several wild "problem" bears amble around a landscaped 2-acre enclosure. Exhibits cover bear biology, behavior, and habitat needs.

From West Yellowstone, take US 191/287 north. After 8 miles turn west on US 287, where you skirt the shore of ❺ **Hebgen Lake,** a large reservoir that floods a portion of the Madison River Canyon. Many sites along the lake

show the effects of the deadly 1959 earthquake measuring 7.5. Here, the quake tilted the lakebed northward, and the water lurched back and forth, flooding the road, and cracking the 1915 earthen dam. Below the dam, stop at the **Cabin Creek Scarp Area** to see a fault scarp left by the quake. The scarp is a meandering 16-foot embankment where the forest floor ripped apart.

Soon, the road hugs the shore of ❻ **Earthquake Lake** ★, created when the quake touched off a landslide farther down the canyon. The high water drowned the trees to your left, leaving a forest of silver-gray trunks where ospreys and bald eagles roost. As you round the western end of the lake, look for **Madison Slide** on the opposite slope, where some 80 million tons of rubble gave way during the quake. The slide crashed down into the canyon, buried a

Lower Falls, Yellowstone National Park

campground, and killed at least 28 people. It also dammed the Madison River and surged 400 feet up the north wall. Exhibits at the **Visitor Center** ★ *(Gallatin National Forest 406-646-7369)* tell more about the quake.

Continue north on US 287 along the most dramatic stretch of the **Madison Range,** which stands as an abrupt crest of glaciated peaks roughly 5,000 feet above the

17

# Bozeman to Yellowstone

Nevada City store

valley. In Ennis go west on Mont. 287 to the restored 1860s gold rush towns of **7 Virginia City** ★ and **Nevada City** ★★.

Both towns lie in Alder Gulch, where Montana's richest deposit of placer gold was discovered in 1863 by a weary group of prospectors who had been run off the Yellowstone River by Indians. Within two years, 30,000 people were making their livings off the gold. Many of Virginia City's original buildings still stand in a cheerful, doddery line along the town's main street. Some now serve as restaurants, bars, gift shops, and museums.

For more of a ghost town feel, visit Nevada City, a mile to the west. There, the **Nevada City Museum** ★ *(800-648-7588. Late May–mid-Sept.; adm. fee)* takes in five blocks of weathered houses, barbershops, saloons, a working hotel, general store, blacksmith's shop, and many other buildings—all jammed with antiques and old-time merchandise with nary an RV or charter bus in sight. Don't miss the wheezing, mechanized music contraptions at the **Music Hall** ★ *(800-648-7588).* Across the street at the **Alder Gulch Shortline and Steam Railroad Museum** *(800-648-7588. June-Sept.; fee for adults),* catch a ride to Virginia City on a gas-powered narrow gauge railroad.

Return to Ennis and drive north to **8 Norris** for a soak at **Bear Trap Hot Springs** ★ *(406-685-3303. Adm. fee),* an amiable spot with a big pool and a tiny shack stocked with a staggering selection of premium beers. For a pleasant hike through a wilderness canyon, head east 10 miles on Mont. 84 to **Bear Trap Canyon** ★, a 1,500-foot gorge cut through granitic rock by the frothing Madison River. A favorite white-water run and an excellent fishing hole, the canyon is part of the Lee Metcalf Wilderness.

Farther north, tour the large limestone cave system at **9 Lewis and Clark Caverns State Park** ★ *(Mont. 2. 406-287-3541. Caverns May-Sept. only; adm. fee).* Narrow passageways connect chambers hung with beautiful formations.

Named for the spot where three major rivers join to form the Missouri, **10 Three Forks** is a ranching town at heart. Get a whiff of the leathery Old West at **Three**

### A Trio of Pests

In his journal entry of July 24, 1805, Meriwether Lewis complained of travel conditions in the Three Forks area: "Our trio of pests still invade and obstruct us on all occasions, these are the Musquetoes eye knats and prickley pears, equal to any three curses that ever poor Egypt laiboured under... the men complain of being much fortiegued."

**Forks Saddlery** *(221 S. Main St. 406-285-3459. Closed Sun.)*, known for its handmade chaps and saddles. Wander through frontier memorabilia at **Headwaters Heritage Museum** ★ *(Main and Cedar Sts. Mem. Day–Labor Day)*, and sit on the shady porch of the **Sacajawea Inn** ★ *(5 N. Main. 406-285-6515 or 800-821-7326)*, a restored 1910 hotel built for rail passengers headed to Yellowstone. Northeast of town, the three forks of the Missouri converge at **Missouri Headwaters State Park** ★ *(3 miles E on Rte. 205, 3 miles N on Mont. 286. 406-994-4042. Adm. fee)*, where the Madison and Jefferson Rivers join to form the Missouri. The Gallatin kicks in just downstream. At the park you can stand on a stone promontory called **Fort Rock** and watch all three rivers flow toward you across the broad floor of a valley hemmed in by four separate mountain ranges. Exhibits identify landmarks and describe the activities of the Lewis and Clark party, which rested here in 1805 to hunt, to plan, and to make 'mockersons.'

19

Headwaters of the Missouri River

Before they acquired horses in the mid-1700s, Northern Plains Indians often killed bison by stampeding them over cliffs. One of their preferred sites lies southeast of Three Forks at **Madison Buffalo Jump State Park** ★ *(7 miles S of Logan on Buffalo Jump Rd. 406-994-4042. Adm. fee)*. Exhibits at the cliff's base explain how Indians funneled bison to the precipice and how they used their carcasses for food, clothing, shelter, and tools.

# Custer Country ★

**830 miles ● 5-6 days ● Early summer through autumn. The Beartooth Highway closes from autumn through spring.**

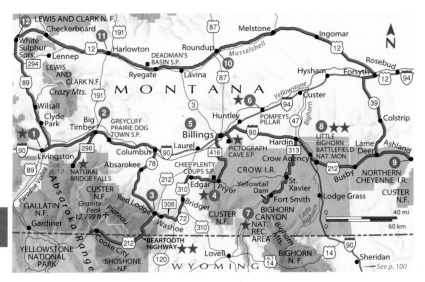

As this tour through south-central Montana skirts the base of lofty peaks and loops out across the grand and lonely sweep of the Great Plains, it takes in the state's highest mountains, the West's most famous battlefield, two Indian reservations, a glorious river canyon, some fine Victorian houses, and a cave complex where prehistoric hunters lived thousands of years ago. Along the way, chances of seeing wildlife are excellent—from gregarious prairie dogs to pronghorn, bighorn sheep, mountain goats, and eagles.

The route starts in Livingston, famous for fly-fishing, and passes through Big Timber, known for its black powder rifles and a lovely waterfall south of town. Then it jumps onto back roads at Columbus and follows them to Red Lodge, where the Beartooth Highway starts its fabulous climb into the mountains, and across the prairie foothills to Billings, where you can tour a Victorian banker's palace. There's a stop at Bighorn Canyon National Recreation Area, which curves through the heart of the Crow reservation, and another at Little Bighorn Battlefield National Monument, site of Custer's demise. Finally, the route doubles back to Livingston on US 12 and US 89, crossing the plains through dusty towns where chicken-fried steak ranks as haute cuisine.

An 1880s railroad town with a lively Victorian business district and neighborhoods to match, ❶ **Livingston** ★ *(Chamber of Commerce 406-222-0850)* stands at the foot of the extraordinary Absaroka Range. The Yellowstone River runs right through town, and Yellowstone National Park lies just 53 miles south via Paradise Valley (see Bozeman to Yellowstone drive, p. 10).

Stop by **Depot Center** ★ *(200 W. Park St. 406-222-2300. Mid-May–mid-Oct.; adm. fee)*, a museum of Western art, history, and railroad memorabilia housed in an unusual 1902 Northern Pacific train depot with a grand colonnade facing the tracks. Then cross the street to the town's famous trout-fishing landmark, **Dan Bailey's Fly Shop** ★ *(406-222-1673)* and watch the flytiers whip together humpies, royal wulffs, woolly buggers, and other bits of tantalizing fluff.

In ❷ **Big Timber** *(Chamber of Commerce 406-932-5131)*, you can shop for a black powder rifle at the **C. Sharps Arms/Montana Armory** ★ *(100 Centennial Dr. 406-932-4353. Mon.-Fri.)*, which builds replicas of the Sharps 1874 and '75 models and sells original Sharps rifles dating from the 1850s. A block away, the **Shiloh Rifle Manufacturing Co.** ★ *(201 Centennial Dr. 406-932-4454. Mon.-Fri.)* handcrafts virtually all of the parts for its replicas of the 1874 metallic cartridge Sharps rifle. So meticulous are Shiloh's reproductions that their parts interchange with the originals. If guns don't grab you, check out antiques at the **Victorian Village Museum** *(110 Frontage Rd. 406-932-4378. Daily June-Aug.; call for off-season hours)*.

South of town, follow Route 298 and the trouty Boulder River through a lush mountain valley that narrows into a spectacular canyon. Fish the stream or stretch your legs at **Natural Bridge Falls** ★ *(27 miles S of Big Timber)*, where

Boulder River above Natural Bridge Falls

the river slides over a limestone ramp, slips from sight, and reappears downstream as a 100-foot waterfall.

Denizens of Greycliff Prairie Dog Town State Park

At **Greycliff Prairie Dog Town State Park** *(Greycliff exit. 406-247-2940. Adm. fee)*, black-tailed prairie dogs nibble on grass, hail one another with 11 distinctive calls, and keep an eye out for hawks, rattlesnakes, weasels, and coyotes.

From Columbus, just down the road, follow Mont. 78 south over grassy hills toward the great hulking mass of the Beartooth Plateau, nearly 8,000 feet above the prairie. Home to mountain goats, grizzly bears, deer, and elk, these dark, smooth-topped mountains are the highest in Montana. A spectacular high-country road, the Beartooth Highway, a national scenic byway, climbs the broad back of the range, connecting Red Lodge with Yellowstone National Park.

❸ **Red Lodge** *(Chamber of Commerce 406-446-1718)* is an 1880s coal-mining town lined with redbrick Victorian storefronts and hotels. Nestled against the foot of the Beartooths at the mouth of a deep glacial canyon, it caters mostly to skiers and visitors to Yellowstone National Park. Drop by the petting zoo and get a close-up view of native wildlife at the **Beartooth Nature Center** *(N end of town. 406-446-1133. Mem. Day–Labor Day; adm. fee)*. Brush up on local history at the **Carbon County Museum** *(1131 S. Broadway Ave. 406-446-3914. Summer only)*, and then head up the canyon for a side trip on the wonderfully scenic **Beartooth Highway** ★★

You needn't drive the whole 68 miles to Yellowstone to see amazing country, but you might find it hard to stop and turn around. In roughly 30 miles, the highway climbs 5,200 feet, opening up incredible vistas of plunging cliffs and gemlike lakes before topping out well above tree line at 10,947-foot **Beartooth Pass.** The road then bowls along for miles over the open rolling terrain of the Beartooth Plateau, where tiny glassy brooks lace endless meadows of alpine wildflowers, and mountain goats amble among the rocky ledges. It's the sort of country that makes people quit perfectly good jobs and move West to sell T-shirts and jars of huckleberry jam.

From Red Lodge head east on Route 308 through **Washoe,** site of a 1943 mine explosion that killed 74 coal miners, then follow Mont. 72 north to Edgar. There, the only gravel road east from town leads through rolling hills to Pryor and ❹ **Chief Plenty Coups State Park** ★ *(406-252-1289. May-Sept.; adm. fee)* on the Crow reservation. The park preserves the home of the last traditional head of the Crow, Plenty Coups, who urged his people to seek an accommodation with whites and adopt farming and ranching as a new way of life. His large log house and store still stand. Exhibits at the Visitor Center sketch tribal history and describe life on the reservation today.

As you approach Billings, check out hundreds of antique tractors, steam engines, cars, trucks, covered wagons, and frontier buildings at **Oscar's Dreamland Yesteryear Museum** *(Off I-90 between Billings and Laurel. 406-656-0966. May-Oct.; adm. fee).*

Founded as a Northern Pacific Railroad town in 1882, ❺ **Billings** *(Visitor Center 815 S. 27th St. 406-252-4016)* has grown into a regional trade and agricultural center with sprawling industrial parks, commercial strips, and suburban neighborhoods. Start downtown, where a scattering of Victorian facades cheer up humdrum modern office buildings. One of them, a 1901 Romanesque library, houses the **Western Heritage Center** *(2822 Montana Ave. 406-256-6809. Tues.-Sat.),* where old photos, clothes, crafts, and gadgets depict the cultural history of the Yellowstone Valley. Another building, the old county jail, is now the **Yellowstone Art Center** *(401 N. 27th St. 406-256-6804. Closed for renovation until fall 1997),* which focuses on historical and contemporary Western art.

You'll find more turn-of-the-century buildings along Montana Avenue between 23rd and 26th Streets, but the grandest of Billings' old Vics—the **Moss Mansion** ★★ *(914 Division St. 406-256-5100. Adm. fee)*—stands about 20 blocks to the west. Completed in 1903, the banker's three-story red sandstone mansion gathers in a disparate mix of interior designs, as if the Mosses couldn't decide which of the Old World potentates to emulate. There's a Moorish entryway, a Tudor dining room, and a touch of Versailles in the parlor. Most furnishings are original.

For a good view of the city and a look at more frontier items, head northwest on Broadway to the **Peter Yegen, Jr. Yellowstone County Museum** *(At Billings-Logan Intl.*

Saddle from the early 1900s, Yellowstone Art Center, Billings

23

Musselshell River

Visitors surveying Little Bighorn Battlefield

*Airport. 406-256-6811. Closed Sat.),* set in an 1890s log cabin. For more great views, follow Mont. 3 east to **Black Otter Trail,** which curves above town along the 400-foot-high rimrock, passing Boothill Cemetery.

East of Billings, **Pictograph Cave State Park** ★ *(6 miles S from Lockwood exit. 406-245-0227. Mid-April–mid-Oct.; adm. fee)* preserves a sandstone cave complex where generations of prehistoric hunters sharpened their stone spearpoints, cooked meals, made jewelry, and painted the walls with figures of animals and humans and with religious images. Artifacts date back 4,500 years, but archaeologists think the site could have been inhabited 10,000 years ago.

Consider a short side trip to ⑥ **Pompeys Pillar National Historic Landmark** ★ *(28 miles E of Billings on I-94. 406-657-6262. Visitor Center Mem. Day–Sept.),* which preserves a squat sandstone tower where William Clark, of the Lewis and Clark expedition, carved his name in 1806 among petroglyphs and pictographs left by Native American travelers. Largely unsullied by modern vandals, the rock records a litany of 19th-century names, from fur trappers and missionaries to soldiers, railroad workers, and settlers.

In **Hardin** stroll through a cluster of restored frontier buildings at the **Bighorn County Historical Museum**

*(Old Highway 87. 406-665-1671. Daily May-Sept., Mon.-Sat. rest of year).* Or, if you're in town on the third weekend of June, you can watch the Indians whup the Army again at the annual **Custer's Last Stand Reenactment** *(6 miles W of Hardin on US 87. 406-665-1672),* an ambitious living history production that tells the story from the Indians' perspective.

Southwest of Hardin, follow the Bighorn River through the prairie heart of the Crow reservation to Yellowtail Dam, which backs up the river to form a 71-mile reservoir, the focus of **7** **Bighorn Canyon National Recreation Area** ★ *(42 miles S of Hardin on Rte. 313. 406-666-2412).*

Gripped between high limestone cliffs, the serpentine lake offers good fishing and sight-seeing, especially for those with boats. Below the dam, consistently clear water flows between the short-grass hills, supporting a world-class trout fishery and offering excellent bird-watching. You can get an overview of the canyon's geology and history at the **Yellowtail Visitor Center** *(406-666-3234. Mem. Day–Sept.)* and sign on for a tour of the dam. Nearby, the **Ok-A-Beh Marina** rents boats to putter around the lake, where you can gape at the cliffs and perhaps see deer, bighorn sheep, bald eagles, and peregrine falcons.

Moving out on the windswept prairie hills southeast of

# Custer Country

Electric locomotive, Upper Musselshell Museum, Harlowton

## Army versus Indians

Though the soldiers who fought under Custer were well armed—each carried a .45-caliber Springfield breech-loading carbine, a Colt revolver, and a knife—many of them had learned to ride, shoot, and fight only after joining the Army. The Lakota and Cheyenne, on the other hand, were intimately familiar with their weapons—bows and arrows, knives, lances, and rifles—and had been trained from youth to fight and hunt on horseback. They were accustomed to fluid battle situations and were masters of guerilla warfare at a time when the Army was just beginning to learn mobile tactics.

Hardin, US 212 leads to ⑧ **Little Bighorn Battlefield National Monument** ★ ★ *(406-638-2621. Mem. Day–Labor Day; adm. fee)*, the site of the most famous battle between the U.S. Army and Plains Indian tribes. Here, on June 25, 1876, Lt. Col. George Armstrong Custer and more than 225 members of the Seventh U.S. Cavalry died at the hands of their intended victims—Sioux and Cheyenne warriors. The battle was part of a war to control the Black Hills, where gold had been discovered in 1874. Miners swarmed the area in violation of an 1868 treaty that explicitly reserved the Black Hills as Indian land. When the government failed to enforce the treaty, the Indians raided. War followed.

Today, a footpath leads from the Visitor Center to the crest of a bare ridge and a cluster of white headstones where Custer and the last of his battalion fell. Other headstones jut from the grass beyond and chart the course of death toward the Little Bighorn River and the site of the village Custer meant to attack. It's a powerfully evocative place, interpreted in great detail and with a fine sense of balance between Indian and Anglo perspectives.

The Visitor Center displays weapons and other battle artifacts, as well as a few of Custer's uniforms and other belongings. Films, talks, and tours begin on the half hour.

From the battlefield, continue east on US 212 through the **Northern Cheyenne Indian Reservation** to ⑨ **Ashland.** There you'll find the **St. Labre Indian School** ★, established during the 1880s and still a center of Cheyenne cultural life. On campus look for the **St. Labre's Cheyenne Indian Museum** *(In the school's Visitor Center. 406-784-2200. Daily Mem. Day–Labor Day, Mon.-Fri. rest of year)*, with its terrific examples of beadwork. Browse for crafts next door at the **Ten Bears Gallery.**

Double back to Lame Deer and head north on Mont. 39 to I-94 via **Colstrip,** where you can tour vast open-pit coal mines *(Visitor Center 406-748-5046. Tours daily Mem. Day–Labor Day, Mon.-Fri. rest of year).*

Jog east on I-94 several miles to Forsyth, cut across the Yellowstone River on US 12, and head northwest into the broken plains, grassy gullies, and cutbank gulches of central Montana. This is lonely country, empty and largely unrewarding except to those with time on their hands and an

inclination to poke around. Still, there's something to be said for getting off the fast-food corridor and barreling across a landscape where nobody cares whether people from out of state show up with a few extra bucks. Most travelers keep their foot firmly on the gas pedal until they hit ⑩ **Roundup,** where there's a small frontier museum and the promise of shade trees along the Musselshell River.

Or they keep on going to ⑪ **Harlowton,** a railroad town with a pleasant turn-of-the-century business district that was rebuilt in stone after a 1907 fire wiped out most of the town. First to reopen was the 1908 **Graves Hotel** *(106 S. Central Ave. 406-632-5855),* a three-story sandstone with a wraparound porch and views of the Crazy Mountains. The creaky old place still packs 'em in for Sunday breakfast. Nearby, browse railroad memorabilia and frontier artifacts at the **Upper Musselshell Museum** *(11 S. Central Ave. 406-632-5519. May-Oct.; donations).*

In the mining and cattle town of ⑫ **White Sulphur Springs,** head for **The Castle** *(310 2nd Ave. NE. 406-547-3666. Mid-May–mid-Sept.; adm. fee),* an impressive Victorian mansion atop the highest hill in town. Built in 1892 from hand-hewn native sandstone and now furnished in threadbare period style, the 12-room château-fortress acts as repository for the county's historic relics. An annex displays old wagons, buggies, sleighs, and local cattle brands.

Take a dip at the **Spa Hot Springs Motel** *(202 W. Main St. 406-547-3366. Adm. fee),* where sulfur springs that gave the town its name flow into two pools.

From White Sulphur Springs return to the Livingston area on US 89, which runs south through the **Crazy Mountain Basin**—a broad floor of grass and sagebrush that sprawls between the jagged crest of the Crazies and the Big Belt Mountains. Look for coyotes and pronghorn moving across the flats and for hawks and eagles soaring over the brush in search of rodents. As you approach Livingston, the Absaroka Range rises to the south and the **Shields River** begins to look like a proper trout stream.

Abandoned buildings west of Harlowton

# Big Open

**650 miles ● 2 to 3 days ● Spring through autumn**

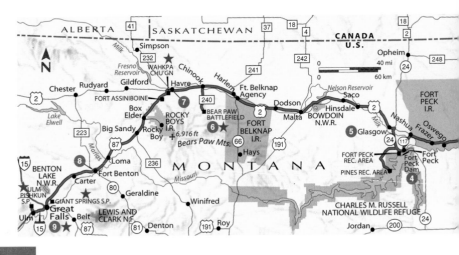

This journey across Montana's high plains stretches from the North Dakota border to Great Falls, occasionally paralleling the Missouri River. Known variously as the Big Open, Big Sky Country, or the Big Empty, this vast land of grass and gleaming clouds is too often regarded by travelers as the Big Yawn. It starts at Fort Union, a reconstructed fur-trading post, then takes in wildlife refuges, quirky local history museums, and the site of the last fight of the 1877 Nez Perce War. Then it's on to Havre, for a glimpse of the Roaring Twenties, and Great Falls, for its wonderful museum of Charles M. Russell paintings and sculptures.

Built in 1828 by the American Fur Company, Fort Union thrived as the preeminent trading post for beaver pelts and buffalo robes on the Upper Missouri. Today the partially-reconstructed outpost is the centerpiece of **❶ Fort Union Trading Post National Historic Site ★★** *(25 miles SW of Williston on N. D. 1804. 701-572-9083).* One of the region's best history museums, the palisaded fort overlooks the Missouri River from a rolling prairie landscape that looks much as it did at the height of the fur trade. Inside the walls stands the gaily painted **Bourgeois House ★,** where

Trade House, Fort Union Trading Post National Historic Site

distinguished guests were feted. Today it's a Visitor Center and museum. Be sure to visit the **Trade House ★**, crammed with furs and reproduction trade items— all for sale.

Take US 2 to Culbertson, then turn north on Mont. 16 and, if you like birds, follow the 18-mile loop road through **Medicine Lake National Wildlife Refuge** *(406-789-2305. Open as weather permits),* one of the country's largest white pelican rookeries. Also nesting in this prairie lake ecosystem are great blue herons, western grebes, Canada geese, and many other waterfowl, shorebirds, raptors, and songbirds.

Animals of another sort inhabit some of the ranches around ❷ **Plentywood**—reindeer, ostriches, elands, miniature horses, fainting goats, llamas, and other unusual beasts. Some ranches offer tours *(Chamber of Commerce 406-765-1607).* From here follow Mont. 5 to ❸ **Scobey** and wander through the **Daniels County Museum and Pioneer Town ★** *(W edge of town. 406-487-5965.*

Deer at Charles M. Russell National Wildlife Refuge

*Daily Mem. Day–Labor Day, Fri. off-season; adm. fee),* a collection of 56 old-timey buildings, most with period furnishings.

Head south on Mont. 13 to US 2 and Wolf Point. If it's the second weekend in July, check out the **Wolf Point Wild Horse Stampede ★** *(Chamber of Commerce 406-653-2012),* a rodeo and powwow where Indian and Anglo wranglers kick up the dust on bucking broncs and bulls. Or catch one of the traditional powwows held in the area almost every

29

Grain elevator along US 2

other weekend in summer. Call the **Fort Peck Assiniboin and Sioux Tribal Museum** *(US 2 in Poplar. 406-768-5155).*

On the way to Glasgow, take Mont. 117 south to the ❹ **Fort Peck Dam and Recreation Area** *(Visitor Center 406-526-3411. Tours Mem. Day–Labor Day, museum open all year),* built during the 1930s as a huge New Deal project. The dam backs up the Missouri for 100 miles, creating about 1,600 miles of shoreline surrounded by the **Charles M. Russell National Wildlife Refuge** *(406-538-8706).* Ironically, the reservoir drowned extensive wetland areas crucial for waterfowl and shorebirds, so the refuge now focuses on upland birds, mule deer, pronghorn, and prairie dogs. To see them, drive to the **Pines Recreation Area** *(5 miles W of Fort Peck, then 26 miles SW over gravel roads).*

In ❺ **Glasgow** stop at the **Pioneer Museum** ★ *(US 2. 406-228-8692. Mem. Day–Labor Day),* a terrific repository bursting with items both bizarre and genuinely historic. It includes the aggressively taxidermied interior of a local tavern with an eight-legged lamb, as well as Indian crafts.

As you approach Chinook, look south across the plains to the dark, rounded hills called the **Bears Paw Mountains.** The landscape has changed little since the autumn of 1877, when the Nez Perce surrendered on the ❻ **Bear Paw Battlefield** ★ *(16 miles S of Chinook on Rte. 240. 406-357-3130)* after a six-day siege that left 30 warriors and 23 soldiers dead. Throughout the summer the

Nez Perce had fought a brilliant 1,300-mile retreat toward sanctuary in Canada. Today a self-guiding trail winds through the poignant terrain where their flight ended.

Four trains a day used to stop in **7** **Havre** *(Chamber of Commerce 406-265-4383)*, a wild town during the 1920s, where thirsty passengers could flout the Volstead Act at 50 saloons and choose from an extraordinary number of bawdy houses. Today you can get a glimpse of Havre's booze-smuggling past by taking an underground tour at **Havre Beneath the Streets** ★ *(100 3rd Ave. 406-265-8888. Daily May-Oct., closed Sun. Nov.-April; adm. fee)*. Also in Havre, stop by the **H. Earl Clack Museum** *(US 2, at fairgrounds. 406-265-4000. Mid-May–mid-Sept.; fee for tours)*, which runs tours to **Wahkpa Chu'gn Archaeology Site** ★, a bison kill site, and to 1879 **Fort Assiniboine**, where a few buildings survive.

Originally the site of an 1846 fur trading post, **8** **Fort Benton** *(406-622-5494)* boomed from the 1860s to the mid-1880s as a busy inland steamboat port. Walk the **Historic District,** which parallels the shady river levee and includes the 1882 **Grand Union Hotel.** At **Old Fort Park** climb into the fort's surviving 1850s adobe bastion. Nearby, stop at the **Museum of the Upper Missouri** ★ *(Old Fort Park. Mid-May–mid-Sept.; adm. fee)*, which focuses on Fort Benton's steamboating days. Nearby, the first-rate **Museum of the Northern Great Plains** ★ *(911 20th St. 406-622-5316. Mid-May–mid-Sept.; adm. fee)* depicts farm life with wonderful exhibits of antique machinery and a reconstructed town.

When Lewis and Clark encountered **9** **Great Falls** ★ *(Visitor Center 406-771-0885)* in 1805, they spent two arduous weeks portaging around the series of grand cascades that once thundered here. Five dams now tame the falls, but the river road is still worth the drive for views of the Missouri and a visit to **Giant Springs Heritage State Park** ★ *(Off River Dr. 406-454-5840. Adm. fee)*, with one of the world's largest freshwater springs. Don't miss the **C. M. Russell Museum** ★ ★ *(400 13th St. N. 406-727-8787. Closed Mon. Oct.-April; adm. fee)*, with the world's most extensive collection of the artist's oils, bronzes, and illustrated letters. Russell's work celebrates the wrangler's life and mourns the demise of the Plains Indians.

At **Ulm Pishkun State Park** ★ *(Ulm exit SW of Great Falls, then 6 miles NW on county road. 406-454-5840. Mid-April–mid-Oct.)*, stroll under the lip of a mile-long buffalo kill, perhaps America's largest prehistoric bison jump site.

**31**

### The Great Havre Fire

Havre's labyrinth of underground tunnels and basements served as a sort of shopping mall for several years after a devastating 1904 fire burned the entire business district to the ground. The cause of the fire is still in dispute, but one tale blames two careless mourners who had followed the local custom of carting the body to every bar in town and hoisting a few at every stop. There were 30 bars in Havre at the time. Dead drunk and duty done, the men returned to the funeral parlor, intending to sit up all night with the corpse. Instead, they nodded off, and one knocked over a kerosene lamp.

# Southwest Montana ★★

**560 miles ● 3 days ● Summer through autumn**

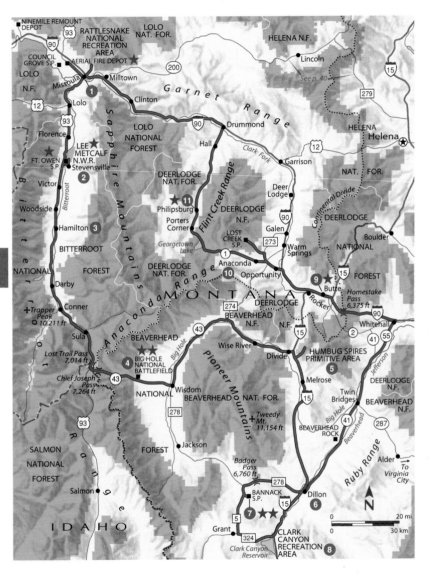

See p. 40

Starting in Missoula and wandering throughout southwestern Montana, this loop of scenic roads strays into the state's mining history. It includes stops at Bannack, an abandoned gold-mining town, and at Butte, known for its sprawling Victorian district, vast open-pit mine, and rich labor history. Other old mining towns dot the landscape, but there's more here than history about hauling ore. The route also passes an 1850s Catholic mission, follows the tracks of the Lewis and Clark expedition, and visits a major battle site of the 1877 Nez Perce War. It knits together all of these sites and more with beautiful drives through forested mountains and spacious valleys drained by famous fishing rivers.

The drive heads south from Missoula through the spectacular Bitterroot Valley, then follows Mont. 43 over the Continental Divide and down the Big Hole River to I-15 and the Dillon area. From there, it follows Mont. 41 north before looping back to Missoula through Butte, Anaconda, and Philipsburg.

Better known for its art galleries and university than its lumber and pulp mills, ❶ **Missoula** *(Chamber of Commerce 406-543-6623)* stands in a broad opening of the Clark Fork River Valley, with forested mountains rising on all sides. Part tenure track, part logging rack, Missoula is an interesting blend of the well-read and the red-of-neck. It combines patisseries, bookstores, and fine art with pickup trucks and greasy spoons.

Start downtown with a visit to the **Art Museum of Missoula** *(335 N. Pattee. 406-728-0447. Closed Mon.; adm. fee),* where regional contemporary works edge out wrangler retrospectives. For more traditional Western fare, check out the mounted elk heads and wildlife paintings at the **Rocky Mountain Elk Foundation's Wildlife Visitor Center** *(2291 W. Broadway. 406-523-4545).*

Near the airport, you'll find perhaps the most interesting stop in town: the **Smoke-jumper and Aerial Fire Depot Visitor Center ★** *(5765 Hwy. 10 W. 406-329-4934. Daily July–Labor Day, weekdays Mem. Day–June).* Skydiving firefighters train and live here throughout the fire season. If called to snuff out a remote forest fire, they must be ready to board their planes within five minutes. Tours visit their staging areas, where 70-pound fire packs, Kevlar jumpsuits, and crates of food and equipment stand waiting for the bell. Photos and exhibits at the museum summarize the history of their dangerous job.

Historical Museum at Fort Missoula

Just 3 miles north of town, stretch your legs and identify alpine wildflowers along the trails of the **Rattlesnake**

**Wilderness and National Recreation Area** *(406-329-3814. Mon.-Fri.)*, part of Lolo National Forest.

On the way out of town on US 93 S, consider a stop at the **Historical Museum at Fort Missoula** *(Bldg. 322, off South Ave., W of Reserve St. 406-728-3476. Closed Mon.; adm. fee)*, a local frontier museum housed in a 1911 Quartermaster's storehouse. Outside stand more of the fort's buildings, along with a steam locomotive, and several other historical structures moved to the site.

Continue south on US 93 into the Bitterroot Valley, where a string of small logging towns lie at the foot of the awesome **Bitterroot Range.**

For a pleasant stroll along the Bitterroot River and a chance to spot white-tailed deer, waterfowl, raptors, upland birds, and songbirds, drive north of Stevensville and follow signs to the **Lee Metcalf National Wildlife Refuge** ★ *(406-777-5552)*. This is one of the few sites in the West where ospreys reluctantly share their nests with, of all birds, Canada geese. The geese arrive here early, gladly usurp old osprey nests, and usually lay eggs and launch their young before the owners return in early April. Sometimes their paths cross and battles erupt. The ospreys dive-bomb. The geese sit tight. Usually the geese win.

St. Mary's Mission, Stevensville

Just south on US 93, turn off toward ❷ **Stevensville** and walk through **Fort Owen** ★ *(Half mile E on Rte. 269. 406-542-5500)*, an 1841 Catholic mission that was sold in 1850 and became a trading post. Partially rebuilt to convey a sense of what was here, the fort encloses an 1860 barracks in good enough shape to house exhibits.

After the Jesuits sold Fort Owen, they reestablished **St. Mary's Mission** ★ *(2 blocks off Main St. 406-777-5734. Tours daily mid-April–mid-Oct.; adm. fee)* on what is now the western edge of Stevensville. Lovingly preserved, the buildings date from 1866 and reflect the clever mind and gifted hands of Father Anthony Ravalli—a Jesuit priest, physician, pharmacist, architect, artist, and woodworker. You'll find many of his works in the chapel and living quarters.

Tepee frames, Big Hole National Battlefield

Farther south, on the outskirts of ❸ **Hamilton,** tour the **Daly Mansion** ★ *(East Side Hwy. 406-363-6004. Mid-April–mid-Oct.; adm. fee),* a 42-room Georgian Revival summer home built at the turn of the century by Marcus Daly, a Butte copper king. With its 24 bedrooms, 15 baths, and 5 Italian marble fireplaces, the house stands on a 50-acre estate offering sweeping vistas of the glaciated canyons of the Bitterroot Range. Daly once owned 22,000 acres here and established Hamilton as a center for his timber interests.

US 93 traces the diminishing flow of the Bitterroot River to the head of the valley and climbs through ponderosa pine forests to the 7,000-foot crest of **Lost Trail Pass.** Lewis and Clark staggered north over the pass in 1805, complaining about hard travel conditions. In 1877 the retreating Nez Perce headed east through this rugged country, hoping the Army would lag far behind. It didn't.

Mont. 43 parallels their route east to ❹ **Big Hole National Battlefield** ★ ★ *(10 miles W of Wisdom; follow signs. 406-689-3155. May-Sept.; adm. fee),* a melancholy stretch of grass and willow thickets at the foot of a pine-covered slope. Here, at least 100 people died on August 9, 1877, during the fourth major battle of the Nez Perce War. After gold was discovered on Indian land, whites demanded that the Nez Perce give up most of their reservation. This led eventually to war and to the tribe's epic and unsuccessful flight to freedom in Canada.

Here at Big Hole, the Army crept out of the lodgepole pine forest across the hollow from today's visitor center and attacked the sleeping village at dawn. After a bloody fight within the village, the Nez Perce drove the soldiers back into the forest. Nez Perce sharpshooters besieged them there until the villagers made their escape.

Start at the Visitor Center, with its fine displays of artifacts from the battle, including Chief Joseph's ermine-tailed jacket, Brig. Gen. John Gibbon's footlocker and field glasses, spent cartridges, weapons, and personal

Bannack, Montana's first territorial capital

effects. Then follow self-guided trails to the village where the Nez Perce families were attacked and to the forested knoll where the soldiers were besieged.

Stay on Mont. 43 and follow the Big Hole River (good fishing) around the northern fringe of the Pioneer Mountains, through a winding canyon and out to I-15 south to the ❺ **Humbug Spires Primitive Area** *(Moose Creek Access Rd. 406-494-5059. Mon.-Fri.).* A nesting spot for various hawks, which glide overhead and screech among the cliffs, this is a good place for a casual stroll or a picnic beneath bright granite pinnacles and swaying pines. Tiny brook trout rise for bugs in the glassy beaver ponds beside the trail.

An 1880s railroad town and ranching center, ❻ **Dillon** *(Visitor Center 125 S. Montana St., in the 1909 train depot. 406-683-5511. Daily May-Sept., Mon.-Fri. off-season)* still brags a few blocks of Victorian commercial buildings down by the tracks. Most of them, including the landmark 1897 **Hotel Metlen,** have seen better days, but the 1889 **County Courthouse** and a handful of grand old houses nearby all look in good fettle. Pick up a walking tour pamphlet at the Visitor Center, then head for **Western Montana College** *(710 S. Atlantic St.),* where you'll find the most magnificent of the town's cow-country Victorians—the 1897 **Main Hall,** a cathedral-like Gothic structure with a touch of Queen Anne.

One of Montana's best ghost towns, ❼ **Bannack State Park** ★ ★ *(27 miles W of Dillon via Rte. 278. 406-834-3413. Adm. fee),* preserves the remarkably intact main street of Bannack, site of Montana's first major gold strike, in 1862. Nestled between sagebrush hills, this double row of sagging log cabins, rickety clapboard houses, and false-fronted shops was once home to 3,000 people and served as Montana's first territorial capital. It was also home to a large and notorious gang of outlaws headed by the local sheriff. They robbed and often murdered people traveling between Bannack and Virginia City (see p. 18) until a band of vigilantes lynched 28 of them, including the sheriff.

Today, many of the buildings are open, their interiors falling apart and aggressively graffitied. The more intact, more interesting places are closed except during tours. A small Visitor Center offers a good run-through of the town's history, and a walking tour pamphlet describes about half of the 60 remaining structures.

From Bannack, either double back to the interstate or make a loop by heading south over gravel and dirt roads to Grant and then heading east on Route 324 to the **❽ Clark Canyon Recreation Area** *(20 miles S of Dillon on I-15. 406-683-6472)*, where you'll find good fishing and bird-watching, especially below the dam.

Either way, return to Dillon and follow Mont. 41 and Mont. 55 north through open ranch country to I-90. In 1805 Lewis and Clark, in sore need of horses, followed this route in the opposite direction. Along the way, you'll pass **Beaverhead Rock,** a limestone bluff that Sacajawea recognized as part of the Shoshone summer country. Her people—and horses—could not be far away.

From Whitehall, turn west on I-90 and climb over Homestake Pass (6,375 feet) to Butte. Founded as a small gold-mining camp in 1867, **❾ Butte ★** *(Chamber of Commerce 406-494-5595 or 800-735-6814)* sputtered along until the 1880s, when new technology and an infusion of capital turned it into the world's greatest copper producer. Mining soon boosted the population to 100,000, created the neighboring smelter city of Anaconda, brought fabulous wealth to the owners of the mines, and put Butte at the vanguard of labor union organizing.

Today, the most obvious mark of Butte's mining history is the **Berkely Pit** *(200 Shields. 406-494-5595. Viewing stand closed when snow on ground)*, a capacious open-pit mine 1,800 feet deep, a mile across, and idle since the early 1980s.

A more cheerful legacy of mining endures in the sprawling **Butte National Historic Landmark District ★★,** which takes in more than 4,500 Victorian buildings—from grand mansions, office buildings, and churches to the tiny, though embellished, homes of miners. Tour or spend the night at the **Copper King Mansion ★** *(219 W. Granite St.*

### Our Lady of the Rockies

The 90-foot statue of the Virgin Mary that stands on a high ridge overlooking Butte was built over six years mostly with volunteer labor and donations of money, equipment, and land. The statue, completed in 1985, reflects the strong Catholic heritage of Butte and offers a fine vista of the city and its surroundings. Tours depart from the Butte Plaza Mall on Harrison Ave. (406-782-1221. June-Sept.).

37

At the World Museum of Mining, Butte

406-782-7580. Tours daily Mem. Day–Labor Day, and by appt.; adm. fee), an opulent 34-room palace built in the 1880s on a half-day's income ($260,000) by William A. Clark, one of Butte's industrial titans. Nearby, visit the turreted 1898 **Arts Chateau** ★ *(321 W. Broadway St. 406-723-7600. Adm. fee),* built by Clark's son. It now serves as a period museum.

Throughout uptown Butte, immense steel frames loom over the entrances to underground mines. Sometimes called "gallows frames," they stand as striking reminders of the dust-and-sweat side of the mining ledger. One, marking the site of a 1917 fire that killed 168 miners, can be viewed from an overlook. Another frame stands over the **World Museum of Mining** ★ *(W end of Park St. 406-723-7211. Daily Mem. Day–Labor Day, call for off-season hours; adm. fee),* a 12-acre site with more than two dozen buildings re-creating a turn-of-the-century mining community.

Perhaps the best way to get an introduction to Butte's mining heritage is to ride the **Neversweat & Washoe Railroad** ★ *(From Rocker, 3 miles W of Butte. 406-723-8343. Mem. Day–Labor Day Tues.-Sun.; adm. fee),* a 45-minute train tour, that climbs the steep ridge Butte was built on and stops at the World Museum of Mining, Anselmo Mine Yard, and Kelly Mine.

From Butte, head west on I-90 and take the Anaconda exit. On the way into town, consider a side trip to **Lost Creek State Park** *(10 miles N via Rte. 273. 406-542-5500. May-Nov.),* where a gravel road threads through a narrow, forested canyon to a pleasant waterfall. Bighorn sheep and mountain goats frequent the high cliffs.

Founded in 1883 as a smelter site for processing Butte's copper ore, ❿ **Anaconda** *(Chamber of Commerce 406-563-2400)* grew quickly as a prosperous company town with loads of tightly packed houses for the smelter workers, big Queen Annes for the managers, and gaudy banks, stores, theaters, government buildings, and a hotel for show. The smelter closed in 1980, and the town still has the feel of a place searching for a purpose.

For an overview of Anaconda's industrial history, start at the **Copper Village Museum and Arts Center** *(401 E. Commercial St. 406-563-2422. June-Sept. Mon.-Sat., Oct.-May Tues.-Sat.),* housed in the town's unusual 1895 **City Hall.** An odd electric locomotive and some railcars stand in

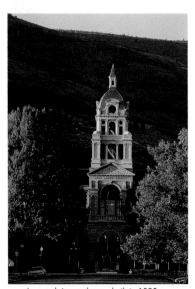

Anaconda's courthouse, built in 1898

Philipsburg

front of the **Visitor Center** *(306 E. Park St. 406-563-2400)*, where you can pick up a walking tour pamphlet for Anaconda's historic buildings. They include many Victorians, as well as the 1936 **Washoe Theater** ★ *(305 Main St. 406-563-6161)*. Its deceptively plain facade masks a lavish and beautifully preserved art deco interior.

Continue west on Mont. 1, a designated scenic highway, through the Anaconda and Flint Creek ranges. The route climbs over broad, forested mountains, skirts a couple of small lakes, dives down a rock-lined gorge and out onto the wide floor of an open, grassy valley.

Soon you'll arrive in ⑪ **Philipsburg** ★ *(Chamber of Commerce 406-859-3388)*, another old mining town with dozens of festive Victorian buildings. Examine Native American beadwork, old band uniforms, fine china, and other pioneer relics at the **Granite County Museum** *(105 S. Sansome. 406-859-3388. Mid-May–Dec.)*. In its dank basement you can feel what it's like to walk through an underground mine. The **Sapphire Gallery** *(115 E. Broadway. 406-859-3631 or 800-525-0169. Closed Sat.)* lets you paw through a bag of muck and gravel to find your own gems.

North of Philipsburg, Mont. 1 joins I-90 W and follows the Clark Fork River back to Missoula.

## Ninemile Remount

Thirty miles west of Missoula, you can tour the saddle and blacksmith shops, corrals, and barn of the **Ninemile Remount Depot** (Follow signs from Ninemile exit off I-90. 406-626-5201. Mem. Day–Labor Day), a 1930s U.S. Forest Service facility that provided horses, mules, and experienced packers for fire fighting and trail maintenance in the northern Rockies. You'll also find some pleasant hiking and mountain-biking trails nearby.

# Glacier and the Flathead

**650 miles ● 4-5 days ● Early summer to autumn ● Parts of Glacier National Park's Going-to-the-Sun Road often closed Nov. to June. Information: 406-888-5441**

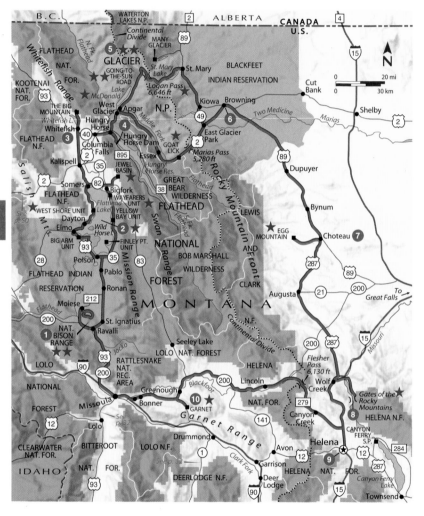

This sprawling loop through north-central Montana takes in some of the most outstanding alpine scenery in the Rockies—Glacier National Park—and offers one of the region's best bets for seeing wildlife. As you drive by the soaring peaks, rolling prairies, forested river valleys, and huge mountain lakes, you're likely to see bison, grizzly bears, black bears, mountain goats, bighorn sheep, eagles, ospreys, and many less unusual animals.

The route climbs from Missoula into the Flathead Valley, with a stop at the National Bison Range before working up the shore of Flathead Lake and heading for Glacier. It tours the park via Going-to-the-Sun Road, then runs south along the fringe of the Great Plains to Helena,

Flathead Lake

before turning west to Missoula. Though mainly a scenic drive, the route also includes a few museums of pioneer and Native American history, some splendid Victorian neighborhoods, a dinosaur dig, and a ghost town.

Start on I-90 west of **Missoula** (see Southwest Montana drive, p. 32), then turn north on US 93/Mont. 200. Soon you'll pick up the Jocko River, which leads through a lovely valley of grass and rolling hills. In the late 1880s small herds of bison roamed valleys like this throughout the Great Plains. Soon slaughtered to the brink of extinction, these magnificent animals survived only because of intense conservation efforts and the establishment of refuges such as the ❶ **National Bison Range ★ ★** *(W on Mont. 200 from Ravalli, follow signs. 406-644-2211. Adm. fee).*

With the abrupt wall of the awesome Mission Range as a backdrop, the range protects 350 to 500 bison on rolling prairie hills overlooking a valley. The bison stump along, their massive woolly heads lowered to graze, their quirt-like tails switching flies from remarkably trim hindquarters.

# Glacier and the Flathead Valley

Browse the visitor exhibits and pick up a map for the 19-mile tour route that circles the refuge, climbs 2,000 feet and offers incredible vistas of the Mission Valley. Along the way, you're likely to see cows and calves in herds, great solitary bulls, and perhaps a few of the animals rolling in the dust or fording a stream. Also keep an eye out for elk, deer, pronghorn, bighorn sheep, and hawks.

Return to Ravalli and head north on US 93 over the open floor of the Mission Valley to **St. Ignatius Mission National Historic Site** ★ *(Off US 93. 406-745-2768)*. Here, in the Flathead Indian Reservation, you'll find the 1854 log home of the Jesuits who established this mission among the Salish, Kootenai, and Pend d'Oreille Indians (a.k.a. Flatheads). Nearby stands an 1891 redbrick church built in high Victorian Gothic style and decorated with 58 remarkable murals painted by the mission school's cook and handyman. Just down the road, admire the work of Native American artists at **Doug Allard's Flathead Indian Museum and Trading Post** *(St. Ignatius. 406-745-2951)*.

Farther north, in Pablo, the **People's Center** ★ *(406-675-0160. Daily April-Sept., Mon.-Fri. Oct.-March; adm. fee)* interprets the region's past and present through Native American eyes. Exhibits and especially tours of the reservation focus on artists, history, culture, and wildlife.

Just south of **Polson** *(Chamber of Commerce 406-883-5969)*, the road crests a large glacial moraine, and the great sparkling surface of ❷ **Flathead Lake** ★ stretches into the distance. Cradled by bulging, forested ridges and dotted with islands, Flathead is the largest natural freshwater lake in the West. Clean, deep, inviting, it's warm enough for swimming in summer, and big enough for large boats. Marinas, state parks, and little resort towns ring the shoreline. Bald eagles and ospreys roost in the pines and glide over the water for trout. The lake also moderates the local climate, allowing the growth of sweet cherries and grapes.

In Polson you can book a cruise on the **KwaTaqNuk Princess** *(406-883-2448. Mid-June–mid-Sept.; fee)*, or dawdle among a feast of oddball relics at the **Miracle of America Museum and Historic Village** ★ *(58176 US 93. 406-883-6804. Adm. fee)*. Jammed with Americana and perked up with a sense of humor, this hodgepodge of buildings houses such disparate items as a "Hotsi Nazi" Hitler pincushion, a sheep-powered cream separator, vintage autos, and a motorized toboggan.

From Polson you have a choice
between heading east around Flathead
Lake on Mont. 35 or continuing west on
US 93. Both sides have much to offer.
On the east shore you pass three units
of **Flathead Lake State Park** *(406-752-
5501)*: **Finley Point** *(406-887-2715. Adm.
fee)*, which occupies a narrow, forested
peninsula; **Yellow Bay** *(406-837-4196.
Adm. fee)*, within sniffing distance of the
cherry blossoms in season; and **Wayfar-
ers** ★ *(406-837-4196. Adm. fee)*, with
trails on cliffs overlooking the water.

Whitefish–The Big Mountain chairlift

43

In **Bigfork** *(Chamber of Commerce 406-
837-5888)*, pipe yourself aboard a
restored 1929 Q-class sloop *(Questa Sailing Charters 406-837-5569. Mid-June–mid-
Sept.; adm. fee)* and sail across the lake as
sunset touches the Mission mountains.
Or wander among the alpine lakes and wildflower meadows of **Jewel Basin Hiking Area** ★ *(Via Mont. 83, Echo Lake,
and Jewel Basin Rds. 406-755-5401)*, set aside for day trippers.

As you follow Mont. 82 across the north shore, look
for nesting ospreys and waterfowl. In **Somers** you can
board yet another excursion vessel for a motorized cruise
*(Far West Excursions 406-857-3203. Mid-June–mid-Sept.; fee)*.

If you choose the western shore of Flathead Lake,
you'll find vineyards as well as units of Flathead Lake
State Park. On US 93 you first pass the **Big Arm** *(406-849-
5255. Adm. fee)* unit, a narrow string of beachy campsites
shaded by ponderosa pines. In Dayton sip a glass of bub-
bly at **Mission Mountain Winery** *(US 93. 406-849-5524.
May-Oct.)*, which grows grapes locally for its ruby cham-
pagne. Dayton overlooks Big Arm Bay and **Wild Horse
Island** *(406-752-5501)*—a state park unit noted for its
knobby upland prairies, bighorn sheep, wild horses, deer,
eagles, and falcons. If you didn't bring your own boat,
you'll have to rent one in town to reach the island.

Farther north on US 93, smooth rock outcroppings rise
above the water at **West Shore** ★ *(406-844-3901. Adm. fee)*,
another state park unit offering terrific views across the
lake to the Swan and Mission mountains.

North of Flathead Lake, follow US 93 through **Kalispell**
(see Kalispell to the Panhandle drive, p. 50) to the resort

# Glacier and the Flathead Valley

View from Going-to-the-Sun Road, Glacier National Park

town of ❸ **Whitefish** *(Chamber of Commerce 406-862-3501)*, founded in 1893 as a division point along the Great Northern Railway. The railroad's massive historic depot, still in use, resembles a rather unkempt Swiss château.

For a panoramic view of Flathead Lake, the mountains of Glacier National Park, and the Canadian Rockies, ride the ski lift at **The Big Mountain** *(8 miles N of Whitefish. 406-862-2900. Fee)*. It operates all summer and winter to hoist hikers, mountain bikers, and skiers 2,300 vertical feet to the Summit House Restaurant. Several trails lead back down.

Next, head south from Whitefish and take the Mont. 40 cutoff to US 2. A few miles beyond Columbia Falls, you follow the broad turquoise waters of the **Flathead River** through Badrock Canyon. The various forks of the Flathead reach far back into Glacier National Park's wild lands and into the vast wilderness areas to the southeast. Portions of these forks form the **Flathead Wild and Scenic River** system. From Hungry Horse follow the river's South Fork along plunging cliffs to ❹ **Hungry Horse Dam** *(Follow signs. 406-387-5241)*, which rises 564 feet above a canyon and impounds a 34-mile-long reservoir that snakes back into the forests and mountains. A very rough road loops around the end of the reservoir, offering access to the **Great Bear** and **Bob Marshall Wilderness Areas.**

❺ **Glacier National Park** ★ ★ *(406-888-5441. Adm. fee)*, part of Waterton-Glacier International Peace Park, takes in a glorious sprawl of jagged peaks, knife-edged ridges, and soaring cliffs that burst from dark evergreen forests, and

tower above alpine lakes and glacial valleys. Rivers and streams of swirling turquoise sweep through mossy chasms of bloodred rock. Ribbonlike waterfalls spill from the crags. And grizzly bears, black bears, wolves, mountain lions, mountain goats, bighorn sheep, elk, deer, and moose roam the park in such numbers that even casual visitors can expect to spot something.

Laced with a fine network of trails, spanned by one of America's most spectacular highways, and adorned with a handful of historic timber-and-stone lodges, Glacier is a joy.

Enter the park from West Glacier and get your first good view of the mountains from Apgar at the foot of long, narrow **Lake McDonald ★.** Stroll the beach and note the distant mountain crest walling off the valley. That's the **Garden Wall,** birthplace of an immense glacier that gouged out lake and valley. It's also the approximate midpoint of **Going-to-the-Sun Road ★ ★,** which starts near Apgar and offers the only road through the park, weather permitting.

Follow this road along the lake through a veil of cedar and hemlock. Numerous turnouts mark secluded pebble beaches that make excellent picnic and wading spots. Drop in at **Lake McDonald Lodge** *(602-207-6000. June-Sept.)* for a ranger-guided cruise of the lake *(fee),* or simply to admire its log lobby and immense hearth.

Above the lake, check out **McDonald Falls,** then head for the cathedral hush of **Trail of the Cedars ★,** which meanders one-half mile through an ancient climax forest of western red cedars, hemlocks, and black cottonwoods. Here, too, Avalanche Creek whirls as a ribbon of sapphire through a narrow gorge of red mudstone.

If, like most people, you can't get enough of that blue water and red rock, stop up the road at **Red Rock Point ★,** where McDonald Creek pools beside great tilted blocks of red stone and mountains rise 5,000 feet above the current.

## Rambling Bob Marshall

A tireless conservationist, best-selling author, and senior Forest Service official in the late 1930s, Bob Marshall is credited with adding 5.4 million acres to the nation's wilderness system. He was a passionate outdoorsman and a legendary hiker who often rambled 30 miles or more in a day and clocked several day hikes of 70 miles. He died of a heart attack in 1939 at age 38. The 950,000-acre tract south of Glacier that now bears his name would have pleased him. Known locally as "The Bob," it extends for 60 miles along the Continental Divide and offers plenty of room to roam.

45

Beached canoe at Lake McDonald, Glacier N.P.

# Glacier and the Flathead Valley

Many Glacier area, Glacier National Park

Cones on fir tree

## Glacier's Programs

Glacier's interpretive programs include guided nature walks, boat trips, and campfire talks. In the **Lake McDonald** area, look for daily nature walks to Avalanche Lake and Sacred Dancing Cascade, guided boat trips from Lake McDonald Lodge, and evening programs at Lake McDonald Lodge as well as at Avalanche, Apgar, and Fish Creek campgrounds. At **Logan Pass,** guided hikes lead to Hidden Lake Overlook and Haystack Butte, and naturalists give frequent talks about the alpine environment. In the **St. Mary** area, take a cruise from the Rising Sun dock and stroll with a naturalist to St. Mary Falls. Guided excursions in the **Many Glacier** area include a half-day hike to Red Rock Falls and a boating and hiking trip to Grinnell Glacier. Call for information 406-888-5441.

Soon, the road makes a tight switchback and climbs just below the Garden Wall to **Logan Pass** ★, on the Continental Divide. At 6,646 feet, the pass lies above the forests and opens up dazzling vistas of mountain ranges, entire valleys, and vast alpine meadows. It's also one of the best places in the park to see mountain goats. You might spot them from the road, but the safest bet is the 1.5-mile trail from the Visitor Center to the **Hidden Lake Overlook,** which ends at the rim of a spectacular hanging valley. Poke along yourself or join a ranger for a guided walk.

From Logan Pass the road hugs nearly vertical cliffs and slants back into the forests. You won't find cedar and hemlock here on the park's colder, higher, drier east side. On the way down, pull over at the **Jackson Glacier Turnout** to see one of the park's 50 small but active glaciers.

Then it's on to windy **St. Mary Lake,** 292 feet deep and ringed with widely spaced, glacially carved peaks. Trails at the head of the lake lead to three lovely cascades **(Baring Falls, St. Mary Falls,** and **Virginia Falls)** and to **Sun Point** ★, which offers a commanding view of the mountains and a peaks-finder chart to help identify them. Boat cruises depart from the dock at **Rising Sun.**

Going-to-the-Sun Road ends in St. Mary, but consider a side trip north to the **Many Glacier** area, where a string of lakes nestles in a glacially carved basin surrounded by peaks. In the heart of the scenery stands the sprawling, Swiss-style **Many Glacier Hotel** ★ *(602-207-6000. June–early Sept.),* built in 1914-15 by the Great Northern Railway from native stone and massive logs.

From St. Mary head south on US 89 to Kiowa, then pick

up Mont. 49, a narrow white-knuckler that winds through spectacular mountain scenery. It passes the **Two Medicine Valley,** a glacial basin just a shade less dramatic than Many Glacier, and ends in **East Glacier Park.**

Here you'll find the **Glacier Park Lodge** ★ *(602-207-6000. Late May–late Sept.),* another gracious legacy of the Great Northern Railway. It was built in 1912-13 on a post-and-beam frame of massive unpeeled logs cut from cedar and Douglas-fir trees 500 to 800 years old. The biggest members stand as columns in the hotel's airy three-story lobby.

When the Logan Pass section of Going-to-the-Sun Road shuts down in winter, US 2 provides the only link between the east and west sides of the park. Largely a canyon drive, it skirts Glacier's southern border and, west of Marias Pass, follows the Middle Fork of the Flathead River through a national wild and scenic river corridor. Views of the mountains are fleeting, but the powerful Middle Fork makes the drive worthwhile.

47

Along the way, put your feet up at the **Izaak Walton Inn** ★ *(Essex. 406-888-5700).* Built in 1939 to house railway crews, the snug, wood-paneled lodge is stuffed with railroad mementos and has the feel of an old, family-run gasthaus in the Austrian Alps.

At the **Goat Lick Overlook** ★ *(About 15 miles W of Marias Pass)* during late June and July dozens of shaggy white mountain goats gather along the river to lap at a mineral-rich embankment of gray clay. A short asphalt path leads to a viewing stand above the river.

East of the park, the **Blackfeet Indian Reservation** spills away from the mountains and stretches across the Great Plains as far as Cut Bank. During the 19th century this was prime bison country, fiercely defended by the Blackfeet. In

❻ **Browning,** the **Museum of the Plains Indian** ★ *(Jct. of US 2 and 89. 406-338-2230. Closed weekends Oct.-May)* exhibits traditional clothing, weapons,

JAMES RANDKLEV

Interior of Glacier Park Lodge

tools, and ceremonial gear—all beautifully decorated with feathers, furs, colorful beads, and woven porcupine quills.

South of Browning, US 89 bounds over prairie hills and roughly parallels the leading edge of the **Rocky Mountain Front,** an overthrust belt of mountain ranges that extends from Helena to Canada and as far west as Kalispell. Huge, wild, and largely inaccessible except on foot or horseback, the overthrust region gathers Glacier National Park, three wilderness areas, and several national forests into an ecosystem larger than Delaware and Rhode Island.

The first dinosaur nests discovered in North America lie in the badlands west of **7 Choteau.** The area still yields dinosaur bones, and there are several digs active during summer. Pull on a broad-brimmed hat and get a free tour of

Kayaker gliding across Swiftcurrent Lake, Glacier National Park

the most notable nesting site, **Egg Mountain** ★ *(12 miles W on Bellview Rd. 406-994-6618. June 25-Aug. 20 at 2 p.m. only).* Or sign up for a multiday paleontology seminar through either the **Museum of the Rockies** *(Bozeman. 406-994-6618. Fee)* or Choteau's **Old Trail Museum** *(823 N. Main. 406-466-5332. Fee),* which doubles as a local history museum.

From Choteau follow US 287 south to I-15 and take the exit for **8 Gates of the Rocky Mountains** ★, where the Missouri River laps against the walls of a narrow gorge. Named by Meriwether Lewis in 1805, the gorge forms one of the most scenic areas on the Missouri and harbors mountain goats, bighorn sheep, eagles, and ospreys. A charter boat *(Gates of the Mountains, Inc. 406-458-5241. Mem. Day–mid-Sept.; fee)* cruises daily in summer.

Wall mural, Helena

Founded as a gold rush boom town in the 1860s, **9 Helena** *(Chamber of Commerce 406-442-4120)* thrived as a mining center and became the state capital in 1894. With 50 millionaires strutting about town, lavish Victorian neighborhoods sprang up around an ornate business district. Though much of Helena's downtown fell to the wrecking ball, gorgeous old buildings still swing into view at almost every turn.

Start at the **State Capitol** *(Sixth and Montana Aves. 406-444-2694. Guided tours daily in summer; by appt. off-season),* with its big copper dome and huge Charles M. Russell mural. You'll find more Russells across the street at the **Montana Historical Society Museum** ★ *(225 N. Roberts. 406-444-2694),* along with artifacts from every important era in Montana's past, from prehistory through World War II. The museum also includes a terrific exhibit of early camera gear and the work of F. Jay Haynes, a frontier photographer.

Nearby, tour the original **Governors' Mansion** ★ *(304 N. Ewing St. 406-444-2694. Mem. Day–Labor Day Tues.-Sun., Sept.-Dec. Tues.-Sat.),* a beautifully preserved brick mansion built in 1888 for one of Helena's early entrepreneurs.

From Helena go north on I-15 and take Route 279 over Flesher Pass to Mont. 200. This highway follows the Blackfoot River back to Missoula, crossing broad grassy meadows and then barreling through a beautiful river gorge.

Along the way, detour to the ghost town of **10 Garnet** ★ *(Signs about 10 miles W of the junction with Mont. 83).* The climb into the Garnet Range opens up vistas of an enormous swath of territory stretching from Missoula across the Rocky Mountain Front. Once a prosperous little gold-mining town, Garnet now is just a scattering of forlorn clapboard and log buildings tucked among the pines. Pick up a tour brochure at the Dahl Saloon and wander.

# Kalispell to the Panhandle ★

**740 miles ● 3 to 4 days ● Spring through autumn**

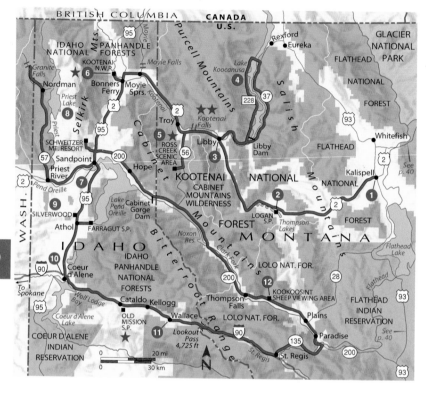

A rambling, mostly scenic drive, this tour meanders through the deceptively gentle terrain of northwest Montana and Idaho's Panhandle. Cloaked in deep evergreen forests, smoothed by immense Ice Age glaciers, the region's mountains seem soft, rolling, even pastoral when compared with the jagged crest of, say, Wyoming's Tetons. In fact just as compelling in their own way, these dark, rounded mountains loom over great river valleys, immense lakes, and a scattering of interesting towns.

The route starts in Kalispell, then heads west on US 2 into the mountains. Near Libby, a side trip hugs the shoreline of a major reservoir, and there are stops for one of the largest undammed falls in the Rockies and for an ancient cedar grove. Soon, the route drops south to Sandpoint, a resort town on Idaho's largest lake—Lake Pend Oreille. Here, another side trip breaks off to the north to take in Priest Lake. Then it's on to Coeur d'Alene Lake and east on I-90, with stops at an old mission church and

at Wallace, a historic mining town. At St. Regis, the route doubles back to Sandpoint via Mont. 200 and the beautiful Clark Fork River Valley.

Founded in 1891 on the main line of the Great Northern Railway, **❶ Kalispell** *(Chamber of Commerce 406-752-6166)* lies along the Flathead River within sight of three mountain ranges and within a 30-minute drive of Glacier National Park (see p. 44). Jammed with summer traffic, swollen with shopping centers and fast-food joints, Kalispell retains some of its Victorian heritage along Main Street's business district and especially on its lovely East Side.

For a tour of the grandest of the old houses, visit the **Conrad Mansion ★★** *(6 blocks E of Main on 4th St. 406-755-2166. Mid-May–mid-Oct.; adm. fee),* an immaculate three-story, 23-room Norman-style mansion built between 1892 and 1895 by the city's founder. Unlike so many other impressive homes built in the Rockies during the period, this one feels as though it actually belongs in the West. Sumptuous, elegant, clearly steeped in money, the house still manages to embrace, rather than disdain, its rustic setting.

Head west on US 2 from Kalispell through the rolling forests and broad meadows of the Salish Mountains to the **Thompson Chain of Lakes,** a series of long, narrow lakes well suited for canoeing, fishing, swimming, a shore

51

Conrad Mansion, Kalispell

lunch, or a nap. To camp, look for **2 Logan State Park** *(406-752-5501. Campgrounds open May-Sept.; adm. fee)* on Middle Thompson Lake.

**3 Libby,** a lumber town, lies along the swift, glassy waters of the Kootenai River. The deeply forested Cabinet Mountains rise to the west; to the northeast are the Purcells. Check out the vintage chain saw display at the **Libby Her-**

Kootenai Falls

**itage Museum** ★ *(US 2 S. 406-293-7521. Mem. Day–Labor Day; donations)* and imagine wielding one of those 4-foot motorized blades on a slick mountain slope. The museum also includes a huge collection of taxidermied native animals, farm implements, and mining and logging tools, as well as a good display of Kootenai Indian artifacts, including a conical reed-mat lodge.

Lake Koocanusa

From Libby, follow Mont. 37 along the banks of the heartbreakingly beautiful Kootenai River—wide, smooth, clear, sapphire to emerald green in its deeper pools. Envy the drift boaters casting for trout, and don't miss the ospreys plunging the current for the same quarry. In autumn dozens of bald eagles congregate below **Libby Dam** *(Visitor Center 406-293-5577. Tours Mem. Day–late Sept.)* to feast on kokanee salmon. The huge concrete dam, built for flood control and power production, created 90-mile **4 Lake Koocanusa,** which extends north into British Columbia along a spectacular canyon of high bluffs and densely forested mountains. An 85-mile loop tour hugs the shore, passing campgrounds and picnic areas before doubling back on a bridge south of Rexford.

Continue west on US 2 along the Kootenai to an

overlook of the river gorge at **Kootenai Falls County Park ★★.** To see the falls, follow the trail through the forest, down a long stairway, and across the bluffs. One of the largest undammed falls in the Rockies, Kootenai Falls drops some 200 feet over a series of stairstepping ledges, ramps, chutes, and cascades. Nothing obliterates road weariness like a walk along the edge of these cliffs, where violent white water crashes into smooth emerald pools and the thundering wash and hiss of a turbulent river fills the air. Downstream, a swinging bridge spans the gorge.

For a quiet stroll among colossal moss-covered cedar trees, head for the ❺ **Ross Creek Scenic Area of Giant Cedars ★** *(About 12 miles S of US 2 via Mont. 56. 406-295-4693),* where a 1-mile loop trail wanders across the spongy forest floor. Often laden with mist and separated by shafts of sunlight, these massive trees stand 175 feet high, with trunk diameters of up to 8 feet. In this exceedingly wet corner of the Rockies, the cedars thrive in the company of great hemlocks, larches, and white pines.

As you drive back to US 2, a terrific view opens across the Bull River Valley to the high, glaciated peaks of the **Cabinet Mountains Wilderness** *(Kootenai National Forest 406-293-6211).* The wilderness area protects a 35-mile corridor along the Continental Divide, which offers excellent day hiking among lakes, waterfalls, steep-sided cirques, and knife-edge ridges. As you approach Idaho and Moyie Springs, US 2 passes 450 feet above the Moyie River Canyon. Just north of town, **Moyie River Falls** drops through the gorge in two cascades of 100 feet and 40 feet, respectively.

Continue on US 2 to **Bonners Ferry,** site of a lucrative ferry during the 1863 gold rush and a thriving railroad town on the Great Northern line. Swing through its attractive downtown historic district, then follow the river out to

**6 Kootenai National Wildlife Refuge ★** *(5 miles W on Riverside Rd. 208-267-3888).* Here, on a flat valley floor beneath the high, rounded Selkirk Mountains, migratory tundra swans pause to dabble during spring and fall. Nesters include various ducks, geese, great blue herons, bald eagles, and ospreys. Deer, elk, moose, and coyotes also roam the refuge. A 4.5-mile auto tour rings the wetlands, and there are several pleasant trails and photo blinds.

Priest Lake, Idaho

Follow US 95 south to **7 Sandpoint** *(Chamber of Commerce 800-800-2106),* founded in the late 1890s as a railroad and timber center. Today, it's a resort town with some attractive Victorian buildings downtown and placid vistas across Lake Pend Oreille (PAHN-der-ay) to the Cabinet Mountains. Dig your toes into the sand at **City Beach ★** *(Right on Bridge St.)* or rent a boat and tour the lake. For a high-altitude view of the lake and the region's terrain, ride the chairlift at **Schweitzer Mountain Resort** *(12 miles NW on Schweitzer Cutoff Rd. 208-263-9555. Mid-*

*June–Labor Day and Nov.-April; fee).*

To reach ❽ **Priest Lake** *(Chamber of Commerce 208-443-3191),* another large, beautiful lake hemmed in by deep forests of cedar and hemlock, drive west from Sandpoint on US 2, then north 24 miles on Idaho 57. Get a feel for the lives of 1930s forest rangers at the **Priest Lake Museum** *(W shore, at Luby Bay Rd. and Beach Trail. Mem. Day–Labor Day),* a restored log cabin furnished with rustic antiques. Then cross over to Washington State and wander through the **Roosevelt Grove of Ancient Cedars** *(14 miles NW of Nordman, near the Stagger Inn campground)* and stand beneath 40-foot **Granite Falls.**

Silverwood Theme Park, Idaho

For a complete change of pace, retrace your route to US 95 south to Athol and the ❾ **Silverwood Theme Park** *(208-772-0513. Mem. Day–Labor Day; adm. fee),* a re-created frontier town with biplane, train, and pony rides; theme restaurants; an aircraft museum; shoot-'em-up melodrama characters; and amusement park rides, including a vintage roller coaster.

A sprawling boot camp for the Navy during World War II, **Farragut State Park** *(4 miles E of Athol on Idaho 54. 208-683-2425. Adm. fee)* lies at the very southern end of narrow Lake Pend Oreille. Hike or mountain bike through open meadows and extensive evergreen forests, or swim at the beach. To see mountain goats, head for the Willow Picnic Area and scope out the cliffs across the lake. Other wildlife includes white-tailed deer, black bears, hawks, and bald eagles.

Continue on US 95 south to the resort town of ❿ **Coeur d'Alene** *(Visitors Bureau 208-664-0587),* which grew up around an 1870s Army fort and became a transportation hub for mining and logging throughout the region. Catch up on local history at the **Museum of North Idaho** *(115 Northwest Blvd. 208-664-3448. April-Oct. Tues.-Sat.),* then stroll through the adjacent municipal park to the beach. Narrow, irregular, bounded by forested hills, Coeur d'Alene Lake stretches south for roughly 20 miles and harbors the continent's largest nesting population of ospreys. A scenic byway hugs the eastern shoreline, but the best views are from the water. Rent anything from a

55

### Camels on the Kootenai

During the 1863 gold rush in British Columbia, thousands of northbound American prospectors crossed the Kootenai River on Edwin Bonner's ferry. Most packed their goods on mules, but a few led camels, which could carry 1,000-pound loads 35 miles a day, thrive on brush, and go for a week without water. They never caught on because most people didn't know how to handle them and because they tended to stampede other stock encountered on the trail.

canoe to a houseboat, or book a cruise through **Lake Coeur d'Alene Cruises** *(City Dock. 208-765-4000 ext. 21. May-Oct.; adm. fee).*

Stretch your legs at **Tubbs Hill Nature Preserve** ★ *(Trailhead at public boat launch),* a forested peninsula east of the beach that offers excellent vistas of city and lake.

Take I-90 east past **Wolf Lodge Bay,** where bald eagles congregate during December to feed on kokanee salmon that have spawned and died.

Often shrouded in morning mist, Idaho's oldest building—a beautiful, cream-colored Greek Revival church—stands on a grassy hill east of Cataldo. The Catholic mission church, now the centerpiece of **Old Mission State Park** ★ *(208-682-3814),* was built during the early 1850s by a crew of Coeur d'Alene Indians working with the remarkable Father Anthony Ravalli. The timber-frame structure still contains chandeliers that Ravalli fashioned from tin cans and the fine central altar he carved with a pocketknife. The Coeur d'Alene called their church the House of the Great Spirit and left it reluctantly in 1877, when forced onto a reservation. Many Coeur d'Alene return annually to celebrate the Feast of the Assumption on August 15. Everyone is welcome.

Overlooking the Clark Fork River

Continue east on I-90 to ⑪ **Wallace,** founded during the 1880s when placer gold was discovered nearby, but best known for silver mines that still produce an average of four million ounces a year. Its splendid **Historic Downtown District** ★ *(Visitor Center, 10 River St. 208-753-7151)* contains one of the most intact concentrations of Victorian-style commercial buildings in the Rockies, and its residential neighborhoods include many fine Queen Annes. The whole town is listed on the National Register of Historic Places. Pick up a walking tour booklet and roam.

While downtown, stop at the 1902 **Northern Pacific Depot** *(6th and Pine Sts. 208-752-0111. Daily spring-fall; call for winter hours; adm. fee),* a beautifully restored château-style building that operates as a railroad museum.

Get a summary of the region's mining past at the **Wallace District Mining Museum** *(509 Bank St. 208-556-1592. Daily May-Sept., closed Sun. Oct.-April; adm. fee)*. Or don a yellow hard hat and take the **Sierra Silver Mine Tour ★** *(420 5th St. 208-752-5151. April-Nov.; adm. fee)*, which explores an underground mine. Like most mining towns, Wallace was famous for its houses of ill repute. At the **Bordello Museum** *(605 Cedar St. 208-753-0801. Closed Sun.; adm. fee)*, tour a brothel in continuous business from 1895 to 1988. Tipped off to a raid, the staff vacated, leaving behind everything from groceries to red lightbulbs.

Continue east on I-90 over Lookout Pass and down alongside the beguiling St. Regis River to the crossroads town of St. Regis. There, the St. Regis joins the **Clark Fork,** and the combined flow brawls away through an impressive canyon studded with knobby rock outcroppings.

Follow the canyon on Mont. 135, and stop partway through for a hot springs soak at **Quinns Paradise Resort** *(Milemarker 19. 406-826-3150)* or for a plunge in the cool river. Soon, the Clark Fork makes a tight bend to the northwest and breaks into a spacious valley, where it picks up the Flathead River and Mont. 200.

The drive from Paradise to Lake Pend Oreille on Mont. 200 is one of the finest scenic drives in the Rockies. It follows the Clark Fork—by now a grand sheet of restless blue—through a vast, grassy corridor lined with forested ridges and bulky mountains rising 3,000 to 4,000 feet. A huge landscape, powerful and smooth, its graceful, rounded lines swell the heart rather than drop the jaw.

About 10 miles west of Plains, start looking for bighorn sheep among the rock outcroppings and meadows beside the road. From mid-November through May, the sheep gather near the valley floor in herds of up to 100 animals. Read about them at the ⑫ **KooKooSint Sheep Viewing Area** *(Roadside pullout 8 miles E of Thompson Falls)*.

Below **Thompson Falls,** the Clark Fork stalls out in long, serpentine reservoirs created by three dams, the last of which plugged the spectacularly rugged **Cabinet Gorge,** portions of which are still visible below the dam.

After reentering Idaho, the highway wraps around the north shore of Lake Pend Oreille, offering fine views of the lake, with its humpbacked peninsulas and islands, and the jagged crest of the Cabinet Mountains rising to the east.

# Moscow Circle ★

**275 miles ● 1-2 days ● Late spring through autumn**

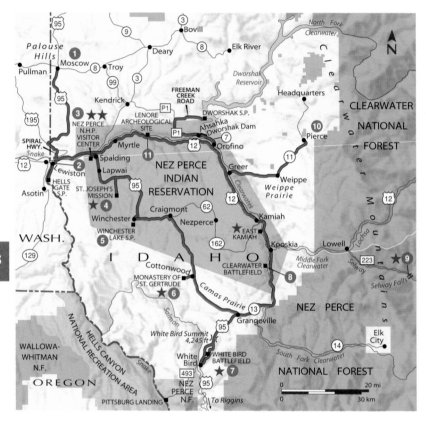

This relatively short loop through Idaho's lower Panhandle follows some of the most beautiful river canyons in the state—narrow rock-lined chasms, vast desert gorges, forested troughs, and steep valleys. Occasionally, it climbs out of a canyon and skips across a billowing prairie to duck into a forest, meadow, or small town. Scenery alone would justify the drive, but this is also a rich historical tour focusing on the Nez Perce and their contacts with explorers, missionaries, miners, settlers, and the U.S. Army.

The route starts in Moscow's Victorian districts, then heads south across the Palouse prairie and plunges to the confluence of the Snake and Clearwater Rivers at Lewiston. It follows the Clearwater to Spalding and then makes a counterclockwise loop through the Nez Perce Indian Reservation. Along the way, there are stops at the various sites comprising part of the Nez Perce National Historical Park—its excellent museum, as well as missions, landmarks from Nez Perce mythology, and battlefields.

Built upon the open, rolling wheat country of the Palouse Hills, ❶ **Moscow** is a prosperous university town

At the Appaloosa Museum and Heritage Center, Moscow

and commercial center with splendid Victorian architecture. Though altered somewhat, 1890s commercial buildings still line Main Street for five blocks with grand brick and stone entrance arches, half-moon windows, and ornamental brickwork. Sprawling houses ornamented with sharp gables, turrets, huge bay windows, balconies, and wraparound verandas stud Moscow's ritzy northeast neighborhood. Most of the homes are private, but you can tour the 1886 **McConnell Mansion** *(110 S. Adams. 208-882-1004. Tues.-Sat. p.m.)*, restored in period style. Pick up a walking tour brochure at the mansion or from the Chamber of Commerce *(208-882-1800)*.

Farm on US 95, south of Moscow

Track the history of horses in North America from their introduction by Spaniards in the 1500s to the present at the **Appaloosa Museum and Heritage Center** *(5070 Mont. 8 W. 208-882-5578. Mon.-Sat. in summer, closed weekends offseason)*. The small museum explains how the Nez Perce developed the distinctive spotted Appaloosa line by selectively breeding for speed, strength, and endurance. A few Appaloosas may be nosing the grass in a corral behind the museum.

Head south on US 95 over the rolling Palouse Hills to the brow of a 2,000-foot embankment overlooking Lewiston and the vast arid canyonlands beyond. Stop at **Vista House** to admire the confluence of the Clearwater River, flowing from the east, and the Snake River, gliding north from Hells Canyon, the deepest river gorge in North America. Stay on this side road, called the **Spiral Highway,** and follow its hairpin turns down the hills to Lewiston.

One of the oldest cities in Idaho, ❷ **Lewiston** *(Chamber of Commerce 208-743-3531)* was built in the early 1860s on Nez Perce land and became a violent gold rush camp. It has endured as an agricultural supply center, transportation hub, major inland port, and timber-processing center.

If you haven't had your fill of Victorian houses, drive up to the Normal Hill neighborhood and cruise Fifth and Prospect Avenues for Queen Annes. Or stretch your legs on the **Clearwater and Snake River National Recreation Trail.** The 16 miles of paved pathways follow the banks of the Snake and Clearwater Rivers and offer good views of the surrounding desert hills as well as the confluence of these two important rivers.

Hells Gate State Park

Lewis and Clark camped at the confluence in 1805. Today, most campers head for **Hells Gate State Park** *(2 miles S of Lewiston on Snake River Ave. 208-799-5015. Adm. fee),* a powerboater's dream on the Snake, with a large beach, marina, and—perhaps most important—shade. Jet boat tours of Hells Canyon depart from the park's marina and run as far south as Hells Canyon Dam.

From Lewiston, follow US 12 east along the Clearwater River, then take US 95 south to the ❸ **Nez Perce National Historical Park Visitor Center** ★ ★ *(Spalding. 208-843-2261).* Unique among America's national parks, this historical park consists of 38 separate sites scattered across four states. Many sites mark the tribe's early contacts with Euroamericans—missions, gold camps, and battlefields

Church steeple, St. Joseph's Mission

from the famous 1877 war. But the park also illuminates the Nez Perce culturally, reflecting their traditional high regard for the natural world, its creation, and its preservation.

The Visitor Center overlooks a grove of trees on the Clearwater River where the Presbyterian missionaries Henry and Eliza Spalding settled in 1838. None of the original mission buildings remain, but the Spaldings are both buried in the small cemetery.

The Visitor Center also exhibits a dazzling collection of Nez Perce artifacts gathered during the 1840s by Henry Spalding himself and sold for about $50 to an Ohio friend to help finance the mission's work. The collection includes saddles, mocassins, buckskin shirts—all decorated with magnificent bead and porcupine quill designs. There are pipes, weapons, a copy of Matthew's gospel printed in Nez Perce, and a faded silk ribbon presented to tribal leaders by Lewis and Clark in 1805. Unfortunately, these cultural treasures are here on loan from the Ohio Historical Society, which has demanded their return if the tribe cannot raise $608,000 to buy them back. If Ohio prevails, the museum will lose the core of its exhibit, and the Nez Perce will lose a tangible link with their ancestors.

Continue on US 95 south about 10 miles to the turnoff for ❹ **St. Joseph's Mission** ★ *(4 miles S. Church open Mem. Day–Labor Day)*. The small white church was built by Catholic missionaries in 1874, and the grounds once included a boarding school, orphanage, and convent. Like the Spalding mission, it's a pleasant, shaded spot to ponder the cultural gulf that existed between Euroamericans and the Nez Perce. The differences extended beyond ardently held religious beliefs to land use, family structure, language—even food, shelter, and clothing.

A popular local fishing hole and campground, ❺ **Winchester Lake State Park** *(W of Bus. loop 95. 208-924-7563. Adm. fee)* surrounds a small reservoir shaded by

### 1877 Nez Perce War

The roots of this conflict lie in the 1860 discovery of gold on Nez Perce land near Pierce and elsewhere. Whites demanded unfettered access to the goldfields and eventually succeeded in pushing an 1863 treaty on the tribe that reduced the reservation by 90 percent. An unrepresentative number of Nez Perce leaders signed the document, but the government insisted on forcing the entire tribe to live on this smaller reservation. In 1877, as the last of the "nontreaty" Nez Perce prepared to move onto the reservation, embittered young warriors killed 19 settlers. This prompted the Army to retaliate.

White Bird Battlefield

large ponderosa pines and Douglas-fir. It's a nice little oasis, the tangy whiff of evergreen offering a pleasant contrast to the open, grassy smells of the prairie.

At **Cottonwood** follow the signs to the ❻ **Monastery of St. Gertrude** ★ *(2 miles SW. 208-962-7123. Donations),* a beautiful Romanesque structure built of native stone. The monastery's museum exhibits trappings of religious life, including books that date from the 1600s, but its artifacts mainly recall Idaho's pioneer history with mining equipment, farm gadgets, tools, old typewriters, and the like. Surprises include a room devoted to Oriental carpets, Ming ceramics, jade figurines, and Chinese paintings.

Of particular interest are the belongings of Sylvan Hart, who died in 1980 but lived for 50 years in Idaho's backcountry, handcrafting the rifles, knives, copper pots, and utensils displayed here.

Continue south on US 95 through the timber and agricultural town of **Grangeville** and onto the broad back of Camas Prairie, where Nez Perce once dug nutritious Camas lily bulbs. Today, it's covered by wheat fields.

Soon, the road emerges from behind rocks and you arrive at **White Bird Summit,** with the vast and broken abyss of the Salmon River Canyon country sprawling at your feet. Endless rumpled hills separated by plunging

ravines, swales, and side canyons stretch into the distance.

It's beautiful country, but it has a bloody past. The valley to your left is the **➐ White Bird Battlefield ★**, where about 70 Nez Perce warriors routed a 100-member cavalry unit on June 17, 1877. The Army lost 34 men; the Nez Perce, none. It was the first battle of the Nez Perce War, which lasted until October and involved a brilliant fighting retreat across Idaho and Montana as the Nez Perce rode toward Canada and freedom.

From White Bird Summit an old highway winds lazily through the battlefield, and an excellent auto tour brochure describes the action. First, though, drive partway down the new highway to an interpretive shelter perched above the battlefield. There, a fine map helps you trace the course of battle. The landscape looks much the same today as it did 120 years ago.

After touring the battlefield, you can continue along the Salmon River to **Riggins** or explore part of Hells Canyon National Recreation Area by continuing on Forest Road 493 across the river to Pittsburg Landing (see also Boise-Hells Canyon tour, p. 66). If you're traveling in late summer, look for locally grown peaches at roadside stands.

At Riggins the Salmon River pours in from the east after flowing for 180 miles across the largest tract of wild lands in the lower 48 states. Two immense wilderness areas, the **Frank Church River of No Return Wilderness** and the **Selway-Bitterroot Wilderness,** form the core of these lands, which also include several national forests, two small wilderness areas, and a national recreation area. Vast, mostly roadless, this rugged expanse harbors grizzly bears, bighorn sheep, cougars, elk, and other wildlife.

Return to Grangeville and follow Idaho 13 east into yet another river gorge, this one formed by the South Fork Clearwater River. Ten miles past Grangeville, consider a side trip on Idaho 14, which follows the river upstream through a narrow basalt chasm for miles.

Otherwise, continue on Idaho 13 north to the ❽ **Clearwater Battlefield,** site of the second major fight in the 1877 Nez Perce War. Here, an Army unit of 500, supported by artillery, surprised the Nez Perce and forced roughly 250 warriors to retreat downriver with their village. The Army reported 13 soldiers killed; the Nez Perce, four warriors.

At **Kooskia** the Middle Fork Clearwater joins the South Fork, and the canyon widens. Here, you can take another side trip up the **Lochsa River** from Lowell into a deep forest of cedar and hemlock. Or follow the 20-mile primitive road from Lowell up the **Selway River** to thundering ❾ **Selway Falls ★.**

Rafts on the Clearwater River, near Kamiah

The main route follows US 12 down the Clearwater to **East Kamiah,** where an interpretive trail leads to a large hump of basalt protruding from a low hillside. Called the **Heart of the Monster ★,** this rock is the place of origin in Nez Perce mythology, where the first members of the tribe were created from drops of blood from the monster's heart. An audio exhibit recounts the tale.

Continue down the **Clearwater River Canyon**—deep,

narrow, winding, with just enough forest clinging to its walls to promise shade. Aptly named, the Clearwater sweeps over a slick bed of cobbles and large, rounded boulders. It's the sort of river that cries out for bare feet, rolled-up trousers, and a picnic lunch.

At **Greer** follow Idaho 11 up the wall of the canyon and out onto the floor of **Weippe Prairie.** Traditionally a root-gathering area for the Nez Perce, the prairie is also the site of two historic meetings—one hopeful, one tragic. Here, in 1805, the Nez Perce first met Lewis and Clark and gave them a feast of salmon and roots. After the Battle of the Clearwater in 1877, the Nez Perce regrouped here and decided to make their epic dash for Canada.

Road along the Clearwater, near Kooskia

Farther along Idaho 11 is the tiny timber town of ❿ **Pierce.** Site of the first gold discovery on Nez Perce land in 1860, the town has possibly the oldest government building in Idaho, the 1862 **Shoshone County Courthouse** *(Court St. and First Ave. W)*. Elsewhere in town, step into a 1928 log cabin and browse the memorabilia at **J. Howard Bradbury Logging Memorial Museum** *(101 S. Main. Mid-April–mid-Oct. Thurs.-Sat.; donations)*.

Drive back to US 12 and follow the canyon to **Orofino,** another timber town. Then take Idaho 7 west to Ahsahka and follow the signs to **Dworshak Dam** *(Visitor Center 208-476-1263)*, an immense span of concrete that backs up the Clearwater's North Fork for 54 miles. Completed in 1973 for flood control and hydropower, the dam blocked a fine run of steelhead trout and flooded elk and deer habitat. Below the dam, visit **Dworshak National Fish Hatchery,** built to mitigate steelhead damage. Above the dam, swim or picnic at **Dworshak State Park** *(26 miles NW of Orofino via County Road P1. 208-476-5994. Adm. fee)*.

Heading back toward Lewiston, US 12 passes a picnic area overlooking ⓫ **Lenore Archeological Site,** a bend of the Clearwater River where the Nez Perce and their ancestors have lived for perhaps 10,000 years.

**460 miles ● 3-4 days ● Spring through autumn**

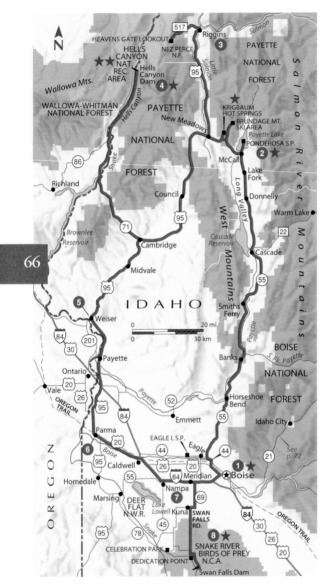

Varied, rambling, mostly scenic, this slow loop through western Idaho takes in more vistas than it does art galleries, more river gorges than fine old houses, more mountains, deserts, chasms, and white water than reconstructed forts. The route starts in Boise, a city rich in museums, then climbs north along a brawling white-water river into the rolling, forested mountains around McCall. There, it tarries a bit to visit a large state park and to simmer in one of Idaho's ubiquitous natural hot springs. Then it's off to the state's western border for a plunge into Hells Canyon, the deepest river gorge in North America. On the return trip to Boise, the route coasts through a procession of small towns and onto the arid sagebrush floor beside the Snake River. And there, a pleasant surprise: several wineries that open their doors and bottles to the road weary. Finally, the route ends at the Snake River Birds of Prey National Conservation Area—a spectacular stretch of river that protects North America's densest concentration of nesting prairie falcons, golden eagles, and other birds of prey.

Built in the desert but cooled by a shady river corridor,

**❶ Boise ★** *(Convention & Visitors Bureau 208-344-7777)*

took root as a mining center and military outpost during the Idaho gold rush days of the 1860s and '70s. Today, it's the state capital, a university town, and home to most of Idaho's museums.

Start at the beautifully restored **Boise Depot** *(2603 Eastover Terr. 208-384-4402. Mon.-Fri.; adm. fee),* now a cultural center, then cross to the north bank of the Boise River and stop at **Julia Davis Park** *(Between Myrtle St. and the river),* a pleasant, shaded spot with boat rentals and a small amusement park for kids. Here you'll also find **Zoo Boise** *(208-384-4260. Adm. fee);* the **Boise Art Museum** *(208-345-8330. Closed Mon.; adm. fee);* and the **Idaho State Historical Museum** ★ *(208-334-2120. Donations),* the state's largest history museum.

Interior of Boise Depot

Nearby, kids swarm the **Discovery Center of Idaho** ★ *(131 Myrtle St. 208-343-9895. Closed Mon.; adm. fee),* a hands-on science museum. Also downtown, the **Basque Museum and Cultural Center** *(611 Grove St. 208-343-2671. Tues.-Sat.; donations)* celebrates Basque heritage and includes an 1864 brick house, the oldest in Boise.

For a close look at trout and their environment, visit the imaginative **Morrison Knudson Nature Center** ★ *(600 S. Walnut Ave. 208-368-6060. Closed Mon.; fee for Visitor Center),* where an artificial stream flows through a small landscaped park. Paths overlook wide pools of lunker trout, and descend to the stream itself, where windows offer sensational cross-sectional views of the streambed and of trout in various settings.

At the **Old Idaho Penitentiary** ★ *(2445 Old Penitentiary Rd. 208-368-6080. Adm. fee),* stroll through echoing cellblocks, some built over 100 years ago and used as recently as the 1970s. Forlorn, creepy, the prison includes exhibits on escape attempts, hangings, and weapons.

If a prison visit seems too dreary, stroll through the flowers at the **Idaho Botanical Gardens** *(2355 Old Penitentiary Rd. 208-343-8649. Mid-April–mid-Oct. Tues.-Sun.; adm. fee),* which bloom just beyond the prison walls.

Street in Cascade

## Snake River N.C.A.

Off I-84 near Boise, a spectacular 80-mile stretch of river protects the densest concentration of nesting birds of prey in North America and possibly in the world. Fifteen species of raptors nest at the **Snake River Birds of Prey National Conservation Area** ★ — roughly 800 pairs of falcons, golden eagles, turkey vultures, and various hawks and owls. During migration, they are joined by nine other species. The best time to visit is in the spring, when courtship and nesting activities are at a peak. A 56-mile driving tour begins at Kuna. Wherever you go, keep binoculars handy.

Boise's premier zoological stop, the **World Center for Birds of Prey** ★★ (*6 miles S on S. Cole Rd. 208-362-8687. Closed Mon.; adm. fee*) runs vital captive breeding programs for endangered raptors all over the world. It offers fine exhibits on biology, ecology, and conservation, but its greatest draws are the birds themselves. You can view Harpy's eagles, California condors, and even get into the same room with a peregrine falcon and learn about its nictitating membrane, a goggle-like adaptation that keeps its eyes from drying out while diving at 200 miles an hour.

Follow Idaho 44 west from Boise and, if you're up for a swim, drive through Eagle to **Eagle Island State Park** (*W of Eagle, turn left on Linder Rd. 208-939-0696. Adm. fee*), a large beach on a small artificial lake with a water slide and picnic areas. Otherwise, turn north on Idaho 55 and climb over massive desert hills to Horseshoe Bend, where you'll pick up the **Payette River.** In late summer, the river flows as an inviting sheet of emerald green past sandy beaches and open ponderosa pine forests. Above Banks, the river's **North Fork** thunders as continuous rapids for 15 miles. In spring this dangerous stretch of white water draws expert kayakers into the froth and cheering spectators to the overlooks.

Tucked into the woods along the south shore of Payette Lake, **McCall** (*Chamber of Commerce 208-634-7631*) is an old, relatively unspoiled resort and timber town. The spotless lake, bracing but swimmable most of the summer, wraps around a long, forested peninsula largely occupied by ❷ **Ponderosa State Park** ★ (*1 mile N of town. 208-634-2164. Adm. fee*). The park's scenic drive leads through forests of immense ponderosa pines to the top of a high basalt lava cliff, where a terrific view opens over the deep, glacially carved lake. Elsewhere, you can wander the park's open meadows, forests, and marshes, or just sit in the shade and look at the glass-clear water.

Back in town, you can tour the **McCall Smokejumper Base** (*605 Mission St. 208-634-0390*), where an elite corps of fire-fighting sky divers lives and trains during summer. West of McCall, get a good view of the region's rolling, forested terrain from the chairlifts at **Brundage Mountain Ski Area** *(208-634-4151. Weekends and holidays July–Labor Day; adm. fee).* Walk down from the top through wildflower meadows, or rent a mountain bike and coast down.

Follow Idaho 55 down a narrow gorge cut by Little Goose Creek and look right for the Last Chance Campground road, which leads to idyllic **Krigbaum Hot Springs** ★ *(Park near the first bridge, follow path up the right-hand side of the creek).* Knee-deep, crystal clear, tucked into a low cliff, and dammed by large boulders, Krigbaum has been called a spa in the rough.

Far to the north and west lies **Hells Canyon,** the deepest river gorge in North America. Rugged, remote, awesome, the canyon cuts a stunning gash through a vast and wild landscape of desert chasms, forested ridgetops, and jagged mountain peaks. Carved by the powerful Snake River, it reaches a depth of 8,000 feet and combines compelling beauty with fascinating geology and a diverse array of plants, animals, and terrain. Much of the gorge lies within

69

At Ponderosa State Park

**Hells Canyon National Recreation Area** ★ ★ *(Riggins. 208-628-3916),* which straddles the Idaho-Oregon border.

It's rewarding country, but it comes at a price. Roads are long, usually rough, unpaved, and steep. You can access the area one of two ways: on gravel roads by going north on US 95 from New Meadows to Riggins, or

Beached powerboat, Hells Canyon National Recreation Area

## Hells Canyon

**70**

With the entire state of Oregon lying to the west, it may be hard to think of the Hells Canyon region as part of the West Coast. But that's what it was for roughly 700 million years. Open ocean lay beyond. Then, about 150 million years ago, the continent began moving west, slowly overriding the floor of the Pacific Ocean. Tropical islands, scraps of continental crust—even whole micro-continents—appeared on the western horizon, moved toward the coast, and were eventually mashed against western Idaho. Today, you can stand on the floor of Hells Canyon and watch the Snake wash over the remains of coral reefs that formed in the Pacific.

travel on paved roads by taking US 95 south to Cambridge and then heading northwest on Idaho 71. Either way, expect to spend the better part of a day getting to and from the gorge.

On the northern route, US 95 barrels down the Little Salmon River Canyon into ❸ **Riggins,** where you can pick up maps and information about Hells Canyon at the ranger station (see also Moscow Circle, Riggins p. 63). You can also drive about 20 miles up the Salmon River, which flows green and clear from sprawling wilderness lands to the east.

Southwest of Riggins, follow Forest Road 517 to **Heavens Gate Lookout** and the **Seven Devils** area at the highest point along the gorge *(check with ranger station to see if open)*. It climbs 6,500 vertical feet through desert bottomlands, prairie meadows, and, finally, a dense evergreen forest at the foot of gnarly rock pinnacles (the Seven Devils). From Heavens Gate, the sprawling vista of Hells Canyon and the Wallowa Mountains seems nearly airborne.

The paved route, Idaho 71, enters Hells Canyon from rolling desert hills, and eventually plunges down into a narrow gorge lined with volcanic rock cliffs rising thousands of feet above the Snake. There, the road deadends below ❹ **Hells Canyon Dam ★,** where you'll probably see white-water boaters readying their rafts and dories for the 32-mile wilderness run to Pittsburg Landing.

Double back to Cambridge and head south on US 95 to ❺ **Weiser** *(Chamber of Commerce 208-549-0452),* a farming and ranching center with a history long and rich enough to boast one of the state's better historic districts. Old buildings in town include the 1883 **Oregon Short Line Depot** *(State St.);* some lovely Queen Anne houses *(Idaho* *and Third);* and the 1904 **Pythian Castle** *(30 E. Idaho St.),* a false-fronted fairy-tale fortress with turrets and battlements.

Check out Native American and pioneer artifacts at the **Snake River Heritage Center** *(2295 Paddock Ave. 208-549-0205. Wed.-Sun.),* which stands on the campus of an old vocational school. If you're lucky enough to travel during the third week of June, don't miss Weiser's **National Old Time Fiddlers Contest★,** a terrific bluegrass bash where tots in gingham dresses scrub the strings alongside wizened old-timers.

Sunflowers along US 95

An old farming town on US 95, ❻ **Parma** stands along the route of the Oregon Trail just a few miles from the site of **Old Fort Boise,** built in 1834 as a fur-trading post. Exterior walls of the **Old Fort Boise Replica** *(E of town. 208-722-5138. June-Aug. Fri.-Sun., or by appt.; adm. fee)* resemble those of the Hudson's Bay Company outpost, but that's as far as it goes. Inside, you'll find a pioneer museum.

Founded as railroad settlements in the 1880s, the nearby towns of Caldwell and Nampa each offer some pleasant backward glances into the Victorian West. In ❼ **Nampa** *(Chamber of Commerce 208-466-4641)* check out the **Canyon County Historical Museum** *(1200 Front. 208-467-7611. Tues.-Sat.),* located in the 1903 Oregon Short Line Depot, a fine baroque Revival structure buffed up and remodeled to house railroad memorabilia.

71

Idaho's desert may seem an unlikely place to grow grapes, but a burgeoning wine industry has taken root on the volcanic ash slopes overlooking the Snake River south of Caldwell and Nampa. Drop in at any of the five wineries and rinse the dust off your tongue with a compli-

Watering the vines at Ste. Chapelle Winery

mentary tasting. Most also offer tours. The oldest, **Ste. Chapelle Winery** *(13 miles S of Caldwell. 208-459-7222),* is especially proud of its vintage Chardonnays. This area is also a large fruit-growing region. Arrive in harvest season, and enjoy fresh-plucked peaches, plums, and apples.

End your tour at the ❽ **Snake River Birds of Prey National Conservation Area★** *(S through Kuna from the Meridian exit off I-84. 208-384-3300).* See sidebar p. 68.

# Sawtooth Loop ★★

● **565 miles** ● **3 to 4 days** ● **Late spring through autumn**

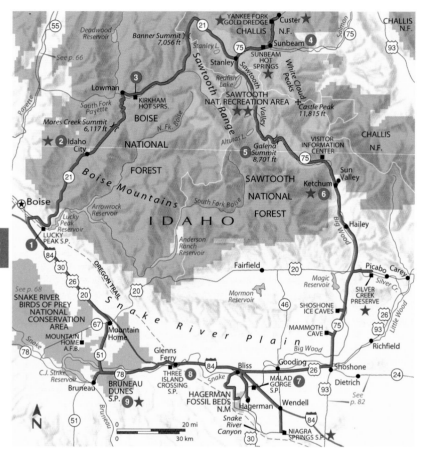

This outstanding scenic drive through south-central Idaho climbs more than 5,000 vertical feet from a desert canyon near Boise into the rugged, spectacular mountain terrain of the Sawtooth National Recreation Area. On the way up, there's a stop at Idaho City, an 1860s gold-mining town, and another at a seductive natural hot springs. In the Sawtooths you can hike, fish, paddle white water on the Salmon River, check out-a ghost town, and look for elk, bighorn sheep, and mountain goats.

From the Sawtooths, the route coasts back down to the desert through the ski towns of Ketchum and Sun Valley. It passes a world-renowned trout stream, explores a couple of lava tube caves, then heads for the Snake River

Canyon, where cold spring waterfalls burst from the cliffs. On the return to Boise, you can have a look at Pliocene horse fossils at Hagerman Fossil Beds National Monument, gaze across an important Oregon Trail river crossing, and hike to the top of North America's highest sand dune.

Sawtooth Range

From Boise (see Boise-Hells Canyon drive, p. 66), follow Idaho 21 east along the Boise River to ❶ **Lucky Peak State Park** *(208-344-0240. Adm. fee)*. There, a high, semicircular dam looms over **Sandy Point**★, one of the best family swimming beaches in the state. Just downstream, at the park's **Discovery** unit, the Boise's cool, clear water swirls through an arid, rim-rocked canyon—a great spot to fish or wade.

Sleds hanging on schoolhouse wall, Idaho City

Continue northeast on Idaho 21 past **Lucky Peak Reservoir** and climb through desert hills into the mountains. As you leave the sagebrush behind and scramble upward into cooler surroundings, the grass thickens and a ponderosa pine forest gathers alongside the road.

You'll know you're approaching the 1860s gold rush town of ❷ **Idaho City** ★ *(Chamber of Commerce 208-392-4148)* when the ground levels off a bit and furrowed heaps of white cobblestones appear on the forest floor. These are the leavings of gold dredges that worked the creek bed during the 1890s.

Gold, discovered near Idaho City in 1862, soon drew a swarm of placer miners. These hard-drinking, gun-toting men worked around the clock by the light of huge bonfires and followed the gold wherever it led—even if that meant knocking over a few houses or a church. Their amazing success (an *average* pan of dirt yielded $1) drew all manner of hangers-on. Soon the population swelled to 20,000. Fine houses, hotels, even music stores sprang up. But the boom didn't last. The easy pickings were gone by 1870, and with them most of the people.

Many 1860s buildings survive, often restored as private homes, restaurants, bars, gift shops, and boutiques. You can pick up an excellent guide to the historic district at the **Boise Basin Museum** ★ *(Montgomery and Wall Sts. 208-392-4550. Daily Mem. Day–Labor Day; weekends May and Sept.; adm. fee)*, an 1867 post office jammed now with mining and frontier relics. A stroll through the **Pioneer Cemetery** *(N of town)* recalls the hard life in the mining camps. Just 28 of the cemetery's first 200 occupants died of natural causes.

Ten miles beyond Mores Creek Summit (6,117 feet), Idaho 21 suddenly crosses into the **Lowman Burn,** a large area scorched in 1989 by intense wildfires that burned for nearly a month and overwhelmed all attempts to suppress them. For the next 24 miles through the **Boise National Forest** *(208-364-4250)*, roadside exhibits explain the fires and their aftermath. With the forest canopy gone, long vistas open up and you get a better sense of the underlying landscape—rugged in the extreme.

Just a few miles beyond Lowman, you'll find one of the best natural hot springs in central Idaho, ❸ **Kirkham Hot Springs** *(Fee)*, which cascades over low cliffs into a series of stone-and-sand pools beside the South Fork Payette River. It's a beautiful spot for a soak—a narrow chasm of bright granite swept by the swift sapphire waters of the South Fork. Pull into the Forest Service campground and pick your way down the short, narrow trail to the steaming pools.

Once thoroughly poached, continue on Idaho 21 as it pulls out of the burned-over area and climbs through evergreen forests to Banner Summit, 7,056 feet. Here, the terrain flattens, and broad meadows push back the forests. Look

## Endangered Salmon

Idaho's Salmon River sockeye and spring chinook salmon migrate nearly 900 miles between their spawning grounds in the Sawtooth Valley and the Pacific Ocean. Earlier this century, thousands of sockeyes and chinooks returned each year to spawn. In recent years, though, chinook numbers have dropped below one hundred. And the sockeye? In 1991 just four fish returned; in 1992 one fish; in 1993 eight fish; in 1994 one fish. The cause? Most of the young fish swimming toward the Pacific die due to changes created by the production of hydroelectricity along the Columbia River.

for elk, deer, coyotes, and hawks as you glide past the open areas and into the northern fringe of the **Sawtooth National Recreation Area** ★ ★ *(208-726-7672).*

This sprawling preserve encompasses four mountain ranges, several large lakes, the Salmon River headwaters, a fine river chasm, dozens of hot springs, shaggy mountain goats, and bighorn sheep. It's the sort of place that begs you to pull over, lock up the car, and put some ground under your feet or a trout stream around your knees.

At its scenic heart stands the splintering crest of the **Sawtooth Range,** a chaos of crags, razorback ridges, and small alpine lakes that extends south for 30 miles. For a terrific view of its jagged northern edge rising over a wetland meadow, stop at **Park Creek Overlook.** Then drive on to **Stanley** *(Chamber of Commerce 208-774-3411),* an outfitting center at the base of the peaks. Harden your heart for the lefthand turn on Idaho 75. It may seem cruel to leave the mountains behind so soon, but it's only for a while, and the approaching plunge into the Salmon River's first chasm is worth it.

The road pitches down a forested gorge studded with granite outcroppings and follows the swift, clean Salmon

Rafters near Sunbeam

as it drops 15 feet to the mile—charging through boiling rapids and sweeping past several hot springs. The largest and best known, **Sunbeam Hot Springs** ★ burbles over the rocks about 11 miles from Stanley. At the crossroads town of ❹ **Sunbeam,** have a look at the dynamited remains of the only dam ever built on the Salmon. Here, the river stalls out in seductive emerald pools warm enough in late summer for swimming.

Marina at Redfish Lake

If ghost towns interest you, turn left at Sunbeam and follow Yankee Fork Road 10 miles to the abandoned 1870s mining town of **Custer** ★ *(208-838-2201. Mem. Day–Labor Day).* About a dozen original buildings survive, several restored and furnished in period style. Interpreters recount the town's history. On the way back to Sunbeam, tour the **Yankee Fork Gold Dredge** ★ *(Mid-June–Labor Day; adm. fee),* which chewed up the river banks during the 1940s and '50s, looking for gold the Custer fellows missed.

Double back on Idaho 75 and follow it south through Stanley into the **Sawtooth Valley,** a broad tongue of prairie that cradles the Salmon River and stretches between the Sawtooths and the foothills of the White Cloud Peaks. The bony pinnacles of the Sawtooths, which reach 10,000 feet, may seem remote, but one of several gratifying day hikes will put you into the heart of them. For maps and advice, stop at the **Stanley Ranger Station** *(208-774-3000),* south of town.

Farther up the valley, follow the signs to **Redfish Lake Visitor Center** ★ *(208-774-3376. July–Labor Day),* a rustic flagstone building with a stunning view of the largest of the more than 300 lakes in the recreation area. The lake, ringed with beaches and lodgepole pine forests, is nearly overwhelmed by two massive, fractured peaks rising abruptly from its turquoise waters. From nearby **Redfish Lake Lodge** *(208-774-3536. Mem. Day–Sept.; fee for boat),* you can cruise to a trailhead at the base of the peaks.

The lake takes its name from the thousands of sockeye salmon that once spawned here. Today, Idaho sockeye and chinook live on the brink of extinction, due largely to a series of dams on the Columbia and Snake Rivers where ocean-bound smolts die in the turbines. Track the decline of these fish and learn about attempts to revive their spawning runs at the **Sawtooth Hatchery ★** *(Idaho 75. 208-774-3684. Tours Mem. Day–Labor Day or by appt.),* which raises steelhead trout and chinook salmon.

From the hatchery, continue south across the valley floor and climb 2,000 feet to the **Galena Overlook ★,** which offers a full-length vista of the Sawtooths. Far below, a squiggle of willows marks the headwaters of the Salmon River—tiny here, but eventually a great brawling river that roars through one of North America's deepest gorges.

Just beyond the overlook, you top ❺ **Galena Summit** (8,701 feet) and tilt down into the **Big Wood River Valley.** Narrow at first and crowded with dense evergreen forests, the valley soon opens up into rolling hills. The river, heartbreakingly beautiful, winds through increasingly arid foothills on its way to Ketchum.

Miners mobbed the Big Wood River Valley during the 1880s, and the gold, silver, and lead they hauled out of the mountains built the towns of Ketchum and Hailey. The towns nose-dived after the silver market collapsed in 1894 and remained relatively depressed until the 1930s, when the Union Pacific built Sun Valley Resort.

Today ❻ **Ketchum ★** *(Chamber of Commerce 208-726-3423)* is a fairly typical Western ski town crowded with gift

Sawtooth National Recreation Area, near Stanley

Ore Wagon Museum, Ketchum

shops, art galleries, boutiques, restaurants, and a crush of expensive new houses sprawling up the valley. The town's historic district includes several fine Victorian buildings and, next to the Bavarian-style City Hall, the **Ore Wagon Museum,** which displays several massive freight wagons once used to haul ore. For more information, a walking tour brochure, or a general rundown on the valley's history from mining to ski resort days, stop in at the **Ketchum-Sun Valley Heritage and Ski Museum** ★ *(Washington Ave. and 1st St. 208-726-8118)*. Then strap on your in-line skates (or sneakers) and explore Ketchum's extensive system of paved pathways, which are groomed in winter for cross-country skiing. They stretch as far south as Bellevue, some 16 miles, and loop through Sun Valley.

Turn left off Idaho 75 on Sun Valley Road and follow the signs to **Sun Valley** *(208-726-3423 or 800-634-3347)*, with its historic 1936 lodge, highbrow shops, and upscale vacation houses. East of town, stop at the **Hemingway Memorial,** a small bust of the writer tucked into the cottonwoods along Trail Creek. Return to Idaho 75 and head south to **Hailey** *(Chamber of Commerce 208-788-2700)*, where you can drive past poet Ezra Pound's boyhood home at 314 Second Avenue South *(Not open to the public)*.

Sacred ground for anyone who venerates trout streams, **Silver Creek Preserve** ★ *(7 miles E on US 20. 208-788-2203. Fishing access Mem. Day–Nov.)* protects one of the last remaining examples of a largely intact high desert, cold spring ecosystem. Owned by the Nature Conservancy, open to all, the preserve includes 2.5 public-access miles and 30 protected miles along a crystal clear, spring-fed creek that purls beneath the grassy Picabo (PEEK-a-boo) Hills. Enormous trout loll in its waters, and fly fishermen come from all over the world to catch and release them. A short nature trail runs along the creek from the Visitor Center, and other trails lead throughout the preserve. More than a fishing hole, the preserve harbors in excess of 150 species of birds, including sandhill cranes, trumpeter swans, and four types of hummingbirds, as well as mule deer, elk, and coyotes.

Farther south on Idaho 75, don a jacket for the guided tour through **Shoshone Ice Caves** *(208-886-2058. May-Sept.; adm. fee)*, a lava tube partially filled with ice. A quirk of geology and weather, ice caves form mainly because they are cross-ventilated. The cave temperature remains freezing despite hot outside temperatures. This cave would eventually plug itself with ice if the concessionaire did not maintain the ventilation.

There are many lava tubes beneath the blistered crust of the Snake River Plain that have no ice. Eight miles south of Shoshone Ice Caves, you can tour one at your own pace, carrying a propane lantern. **Mammoth Cave** *(May-Sept.; adm. fee)* is so long, so large, and its walls so uniformly curved that it resembles a subway tunnel. Stocked as a fallout shelter during the Cold War, Mammoth is worth a stop just to gape at the scruffy taxidermied animals in the entrance office. Peacocks, pigs, and chickens have the run of the yard.

Waterfall at Malad Gorge State Park

From Shoshone take US 26 west to I-84, then head southeast a few miles to **⑦ Malad Gorge State Park** *(208-837-4505)*. Here, you can drive or walk along the rim of Malad Gorge, a narrow canyon that splits the desert floor and opens onto the grand trough of the Snake River Canyon. Start at Devils Washbowl, where a footbridge spans the upper end of the gorge. Far below, the Malad River spills from a cleft in the rocks and rushes down the canyon. Waterfalls stairstep from the rim, and clear spring water pours in from several points.

The springs at Malad Gorge are part of a large network

of major springs that empty into this section of the Snake River Canyon. Sometimes bursting from the cliffs in roaring cascades, the springs mark the terminus of the vast Snake River aquifer, which gathers some of its waters from as far away as Yellowstone.

One of the most spectacular of these, **Niagara Springs** ★ surges from basalt cliffs at a poorly marked but lovely state park south of Wendell *(from I-84 head south 9.5 miles over rim and bear left on canyon floor past fish hatchery).* The spring sprawls over a shaded grotto of boulders into a broad pool of clear, achingly beautiful water. Along the Snake, look for cormorants, great blue herons, pelicans, and many other water birds.

In **Hagerman** *(Chamber of Commerce 208-837-9131)* sip vintage Idaho Chardonnay at the **Rose Creek Winery** *(208-837-4413. Daily tastings),* or check out pioneer and Indian artifacts and a horse skeleton replica at the **Hagerman Valley Historical Society Museum** *(208-837-6288. Mid-Feb.–mid-Dec. Wed.-Sun.).*

South of Hagerman, springs still flow from the cliffs, but most have been diverted, often to supply large fish farms with clean, cold water. About 75 percent of the nation's commercial rainbow trout are raised along this 30-mile stretch of the Snake. Some hatcheries are open for tours.

Abundant spring water isn't the only surprising find along the slopes of the Snake River Canyon. In the steep bluffs across the river from Hagerman lies one of the richest fossil beds in North America. Renowned for skeletons of an extinct horse species, the **Hagerman Fossil Beds** *(Visitor Center in Hagerman. 208-837-4793)* are now a national monument. Besides ancient horse bones, the beds have yielded remains of camels, frogs, rabbits, turtles, water birds, fish, ground sloths, mice—over 100 species of vertebrates so far. All reflect the moist savanna environment that existed here 3.5 million years ago. The monument, established in 1988, remains largely inaccessible and thinly interpreted. On summer weekends, though, rangers often lead group tours to the horse quarry. Call for a schedule.

Oregon Trail emigrants made one of their most dangerous river crossings at what is now ❽ **Three Island Crossing State Park** *(Glenns Ferry exit from I-84. 208-366-2394. Adm. fee).* Here beneath the high bluffs of the Snake River Canyon, they forded on gravel bars that extend between three small islands. At low water, it was the best

Sand dunes, Bruneau Dunes State Park

place to cross to the north bank of the Snake, which offered a shorter route, better water, and good forage for their livestock. Every August locals reenact the crossing.

You can brush up on the lore of the place at the park's Visitor Center, then amble down to the crossing, where the hot breath of the desert mingles with the cool, wet breeze of the river. The landscape hasn't changed much in 150 years, and neither has the refreshing sense of oasis. What a relief the river must have been to those who plodded all day in the dust beside oxen, mules, and irritable mates.

Sensuous, at times even surreal, two massive sand dunes loom over a crystalline lake at ❾ **Bruneau Dunes State Park** ★ *(Hammett exit. 208-366-7919. Adm. fee).* The dunes, connected by a sand ridge, occupy an abandoned meander of the Snake River that traps windblown sand. Though it's a small dune field, it contains the highest single-structured dune in North America—470 feet. Trails loop throughout the park.

Stop at the environmental education center for a look at the fossilized bones of ancient camels, giant ground sloths, fish, even a sabertooth skull—all discovered within 50 miles of the dunes. Today's wildlife reflects the park's wide spectrum of habitats. Scorpions and horned lizards share the place with ducks and muskrats.

# Twin Falls Loop

**390 miles ● 2 to 3 days ● Spring and autumn**

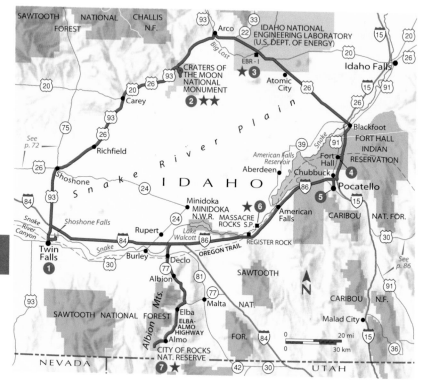

As it loops around the heart of southern Idaho's desert, this drive takes in a fascinating volcanic landscape, rolling velvety foothills, vast sagebrush flats, and the grand trough of the Snake River Canyon. It starts at Twin Falls along the canyon's rim, then glides northeast across the desert to Craters of the Moon National Monument. From Arco it turns southeast, pausing for a tour of the world's first nuclear breeder reactor. In Blackfoot there's a stop at a quirky potato museum before the route turns southwest to follow a stretch of the Oregon Trail. Stops include a reconstructed fort in Pocatello and a beautiful state park on the banks of the Snake. Then, if time permits, take a side trip to the odd granite formations of City of Rocks National Reserve.

In the early 1900s, farmers swarmed ❶ **Twin Falls** *(Chamber of Commerce 208-733-3974)* to grub sagebrush and grow irrigated crops on the sun-hammered desert flats. The source of their prosperity, the Snake River, cuts an abrupt and spectacular gorge beneath their fields, dwarfs the town, and stretches across most of southern Idaho. From **Perrine Memorial Bridge** (*Northern approach to town*), you get a fine view of the void, 500 feet deep and about 1,500 feet wide at

Perrine Memorial Bridge, Twin Falls

this point. To reach the floor of the gorge, follow the signs to **Centennial Waterfront Park** (*Right on Canyon Springs Rd.*), a picnic ground and departure point for boat tours. Back on the rim, head for the **Herrett Center for Arts and Science** (*College of Southern Idaho. 208-733-9554. Tues.-Sat.*), where exhibits depict early human life along the Snake. Farther west, the **Twin Falls County Historical Society and Museum** (*3.5 miles W on US 30. 208-734-5547. Mid-May–Aug. Tues.-Sat.; donations*) displays mementos of pioneer days. Upstream dams shut off 212-foot **Shoshone Falls** (*3 miles E on Falls Ave., follow signs. 208-736-2265. Mid-May–Sept.; adm. fee*) for much of the year, but the Niagara of the West still thunders for several weeks starting in May.

Follow US 93 north to **Shoshone,** with its handful of lava-rock buildings, then head out onto the broad desert floor of the Snake River Plain, where hawks wheel above the sagebrush. Within an hour or so, you'll begin crossing the first of the vast lava flows that make up ❷ **Craters of the Moon National Monument** ★★ (*Visitor Center 208-527-3257*). This coarse landscape—charred, brutal, weird yet beautiful—is part of a 588-square-mile lava flow, the biggest of three that spewed and oozed from the Great Rift volcanic rift zone, a 62-mile wound in the earth that opened 15,000 years ago. The monument's cinder cones, splatter cones, lava tubes, rubble heaps, and great riverlike pleats of smooth lava formed during eight distinct eruptive periods that ended just 2,000 years ago.

Shoshone Falls

By no means barren, the cinder slopes, rock clefts, and caves support 300 plant species, 148 types of birds, 49 species of mammals, and 8 types of reptiles—all of which adapt in fascinating ways to a dry environment where temperatures can reach 150°F.

For a look at lava bombs and other forms of volcanic shrapnel, stop at the Visitor Center, where exhibits and a short film offer a primer. Join a ranger for a guided hike, or head out on your own for the 7-mile loop road that encircles **Inferno Cone.** Its summit, a short steep walk, offers a distant view of other cinder cones aligned along the Great Rift. Spur roads and footpaths lead to other curiosities including **Indian Tunnel ★,** an enormous lava tube cave.

Continue on US 93 to **Arco,** where a welcoming sign proclaims it the world's first town lit by atomic energy, then follow US 20/26 to ❸ **Experimental Breeder Reactor-I National Historic Landmark ★** *(208-526-0050. Tours daily Mem. Day–Labor Day or by appt.),* where you can visit the world's first nuclear power plant and breeder reactor. Here, in 1951, the reactor became the first to generate electricity from atomic energy. The analogue dials and

Interior of Old Fort Hall Replica, Pocatello

meters of the control room lend an odd, antiquated feel to a place once on the leading edge of technology. Outside stand two aircraft nuclear engine prototypes for nuclear planes that were never built.

In **Blackfoot** consider a pilgrimage to the **Idaho Potato Expo** *(130 NW Main. 208-785-2517. May-Oct., call for off-season schedule; adm. fee),* a museum and gift shop where the state's most famous cash crop is venerated and exploited to within an inch of its life. Here you'll find a complete line of designer spudwear, French fry phones, potato hand lotion, and such items of historic import as a spud autographed by former Vice President Dan Quayle. The expo's kitchen hands out free "taters for out-of-staters," but you have to pay for potato ice cream.

To get a Native American take on Western history, stop at ❹ **Fort Hall** and visit the **Shoshone-Bannock Tribal Museum** *(208-237-9791. April–mid-Oct.; donations)*, where exhibits summarize the histories of both tribes as well as what's known about humans who lived along the Snake River at least 7,000 years ago. The old fort, an important Oregon Trail stop, no longer stands, but the museum runs tours of the site.

Tepee at Old Fort Hall Replica

An old railroad town, ❺ **Pocatello** boasts one of the region's most diverse and well-preserved downtown historic districts. It covers some 18 blocks and includes more than 80 buildings of brick, stone, and terra cotta that reflect such wide-ranging styles as Gothic Revival and art deco. In summer, pick up a tour brochure at the Visitor Center *(208-233-1525)*. For an overview of the region's geology, plants, and animals, head for the state university campus and the **Idaho Museum of Natural History** ★ *(S. 5th Ave. and E. Dillon St. 208-236-3168. Closed Sun.; adm. fee for special exhibits)*. At **Ross Park** on the city's southeast side, you'll find the **Old Fort Hall Replica** ★ *(208-234-6233. June-Sept., call for off-season hours; adm. fee)*. A white stucco enclosure with log cabins and sheds, the fort was built in the 1960s from Hudson's Bay Company plans and includes a blacksmith shop, trade room, and lordly suite for the post's factor. Also in the park, look back on local history at the **Bannock County Historical Society and Museum** *(208-233-0434. Mem. Day–Labor Day Tues.-Sat., call for off-season hours; adm. fee)*, or see native animals such as elk, mountain lions, and grizzlies at the **Ross Park Zoo** *(2100 S. 2nd Ave. 208-234-6196. Adm. fee)*.

Southwest along I-86 and overlooking the broad Snake River and its desert canyon is ❻ **Massacre Rocks State Park** ★ *(12 miles W of American Falls. 208-548-2672. Adm. fee)*, named for an 1862 fight with Indians that left ten Oregon Trail emigrants dead. Exhibits recount the two-day fight and map the entire Oregon Trail and its branches. Down the road, emigrants tapped their names into **Register Rock.**

Before completing the loop back to Twin Falls, take an excursion to ❼ **City of Rocks National Reserve** ★ *(Visitor Center 208-824-5519)*. See sidebar on this page.

85

### City of Rocks

Roughly 40 miles south of I-84 through the eye-blink towns on Albion and Elba, **City of Rocks National Reserve** embraces deeply eroded outcroppings of granite up to 2.5 billion years old. Weathered into knobs, spires, and great smooth-faced domes, some of the rocks were given such names as Camp Rock, Twin Sisters, and Chinaman's Head by emigrants bound for California in the 1840s and '50s. Primitive, peaceful, lightly visited, garden-like, the reserve harbors elk, mule deer, eagles, falcons, hummingbirds, and technical rock climbers.

# Bear Lake Circuit

**350 miles ● 2 days ● Spring through autumn**

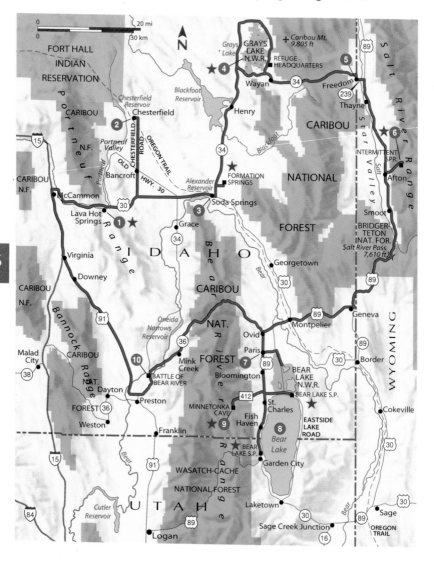

Water, in its more curious forms, tends to unify this mostly scenic drive through southeastern Idaho's high desert lands, forested mountain valleys, and rolling grassland hills. It starts with a soak in Lava Hot Springs, then checks out Soda Springs. It climbs to Grays Lake National Wildlife Refuge, home to greater sandhill and whooping cranes, and stops in Wyoming's Star Valley for an odd intermittent spring. Then it's on to Bear Lake, an immense body of turquoise water ringed with beaches. Other stops include a pioneer town and an elegant 1880s stone tabernacle.

A favorite swimming hole in the desert, **❶ Lava Hot Springs ★** *(Chamber of Commerce 208-776-5500)* lies in a narrow canyon carved out by the Portneuf River. Crowded during summer with bathing suits, towels, and inner tubes, this weathered resort town offers three great ways to get wet. Leap into cool water at the **Olympic Swimming Complex ★** *(NW edge of town. 208-776-5221 or 800-423-8597. Mem. Day–Labor Day; adm. fee)*, with its enormous pool and high-diving platforms. Or rent an inner tube and bob through town on the Portneuf. To warm up, head for **Idaho's World Famous Hot Pools ★** *(430 E. Main. 208-776-5221 or 800-423-8597. Adm. fee)*. Gravel bottomed or lined with flagstones, the pools are large, sociable, crystal clear, and odorless. The biggest lies beneath a lovely rock garden.

Continue east on US 30 over a high ridge and out onto the Portneuf Valley. This huge, flat, treeless valley floor presented Oregon Trail emigrants with miles of smooth sailing as they traveled from Soda Springs toward Fort Hall. The wagon route ran past **❷ Chesterfield** *(15 miles N of US 30)*, an abandoned pioneer town. Its scattering of brick buildings and log cabins are being restored by volunteers.

The geyser in **❸ Soda Springs** *(City Hall 208-547-2600)* is a cheerful fake—an accident, really, unleashed by a 1937 drilling crew. Capped today and regulated, it erupts at **Geyser Park** regularly, reaching heights of 150 feet.

The town takes its name from the refreshing Oregon Trail landmark bubbling from the ground at **Hooper Springs Park ★** *(N on Idaho 34, follow signs)*. The water—cold, crystal clear, with a metallic flavor and fizz—pools under a rock and a log pavilion. Take a tip from the emigrants and mix the water with a pinch of sugar (or, perhaps, a shot of red-eye).

Return to Idaho 34 north and turn right on Trail Canyon Road to reach **Formation Springs ★,** a series of deep cold-spring pools matted with aquatic vegetation, ringed with prairie wildflowers, and surrounded by grassy meadows.

Lava Hot Springs

## Battle of Bear River

On January 29, 1863, near the town of Preston, more than 220 Shoshone men, women, and children were slaughtered by Col. Patrick Connor and his California Volunteers in Idaho's bloodiest battle. Connor struck the camp after miners were attacked by Indians elsewhere on the Bear River. He confiscated the Shoshone horse herd, burned the camp, destroyed its contents, and captured women and children. Connor reported losing 20 men, but won promotion to brigadier.

87

Heart-wrenchingly beautiful, this Nature Conservancy preserve is very poorly marked. Look for the buck-and-rail fence to your left. The site includes a 1,000-foot cave.

About 30 miles north of Soda Springs, **④ Grays Lake National Wildlife Refuge** ★ *(208-574-2755)* sprawls at the foot of Idaho's Caribou Mountain as a large, shallow marsh surrounded by meadows. Home to the world's largest nesting population of greater sandhill cranes, Grays Lake is also one of the few places you have a fairly good chance of seeing an endangered whooping crane. As many as 200 nesting pairs of sandhills begin arriving in early April. With them come a few whoopers raised as foster young by sandhills in an attempt by the U.S. Fish and Wildlife Service to establish a breeding population of whoopers. Unfortunately, the whoopers seem more interested in courting sandhills than one another. While driving the refuge loop road, listen for the guttural chuckle of sandhills and look for ducks, geese, peregrine falcons, moose, elk, and mule deer.

There's a dreamy feel about the drive into Wyoming and **Star Valley** *(Chamber of Commerce 800-426-8833)* that makes you want to push back the seat and flop an arm out the window. Roomy, green, soothing, the valley follows the Salt River through pastoral dairy farm country encircled by mountains.

Sandhill cranes, Grays Lake National Wildlife Refuge

Idaho 34 drops to the valley floor through tiny **⑤ Freedom,** Wyoming, where you can stop at **Freedom Arms Inc.** *(307-883-2468. Mon.-Fri.)*, makers of the most powerful revolver in the world.

East of Afton and up a narrow forested chasm, **⑥ Intermittent Spring** ★ *(2nd Ave. E for 5 miles, follow trail for 45 minutes)* pours from a cliff face for 18 minutes at a time then shuts down for the same length of time before resuming. A rare natural curiosity, this seasonal phenomenon is at its best during autumn.

Farther south, tour the **CallAir Museum** *(S of Afton on US 89. 307-886-9881. Mid-May–Sept. Mon.-Sat.; call for off-season hours)*, which displays vintage lightweight aircraft including a midget biplane.

Continue on US 89 through Montpelier, Idaho, to ❼ **Paris** and visit the **Paris Idaho Stake Tabernacle** ★ *(Mem. Day–Labor Day),* an impressive 1880s structure designed by one of Brigham Young's sons. Built of red sandstone hauled 18 miles from Bear Lake, the building seats nearly 1,500.

Gateway festooned with antlers, St. Charles

At times a robin's-egg blue, ❽ **Bear Lake** stretches for nearly 20 miles, cradled between rumpled desert foothills and a northern spur of Utah's Wasatch Range. Stroll, wade, or swim along the miles of white-sand beaches.

Just north of the lake, **Bear Lake National Wildlife Refuge** *(208-847-1757)* encompasses a large marsh harboring one of the country's largest nesting colonies of the rare white-faced ibis. Other nesters include snowy egrets, black-crowned night-herons, western grebes, gulls, and terns.

Nearby, unfold your beach chair at Idaho's **Bear Lake State Park** ★ *(208-945-2790. Adm. fee),* which embraces two enormous sand beaches and offers picnic grounds and camping areas along the north and east shores. At the southern end of the lake, Utah also runs a **Bear Lake State Park** ★ *(801-946-3343. Adm. fee),* with a large beach.

Returning to St. Charles, head west on the well-marked side road to ❾ **Minnetonka Cave** ★ *(208-945-2407. Mid-June–mid-Sept.; adm. fee),* one of the few large limestone caverns in Idaho. The road climbs through a beautiful forested canyon with fine vistas of Bear Lake. Cave tours focus on trivia, but the long stroll takes you through magnificent chambers of drip rock and flow stone formations.

Interior of Paris Idaho Stake Tabernacle

Head north to Paris and follow Idaho 36 west into Bear River Valley. A few miles short of Preston, a historical marker identifies the site of the ❿ **Battle of Bear River,** Idaho's bloodiest ground. See sidebar on p. 87. From here continue on to Preston, then return to I-15 on US 91.

# Northwest Corner ★★

**525 miles ● 3 days ● Midsummer through autumn.
● Expect heavy traffic in Yellowstone National Park
during summer months. Most of Yellowstone's roads,
as well as Teton Park Road, close in winter. Other
roads may close temporarily during heavy snow.**

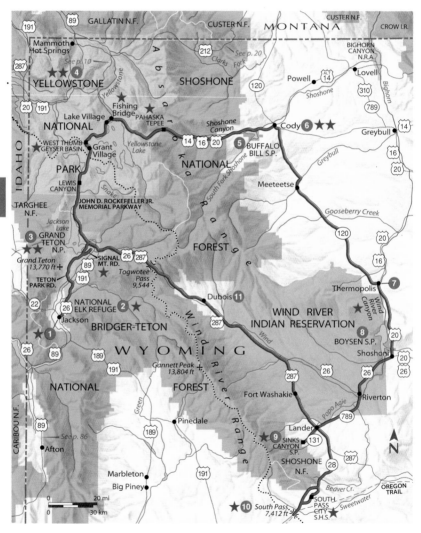

This ragged loop of roads starts in the high country of
northwestern Wyoming among glacial lakes, chilly rivers,
and spectacular mountain terrain. It passes through both
Grand Teton and Yellowstone National Parks before
descending through a forested canyon to the high desert of

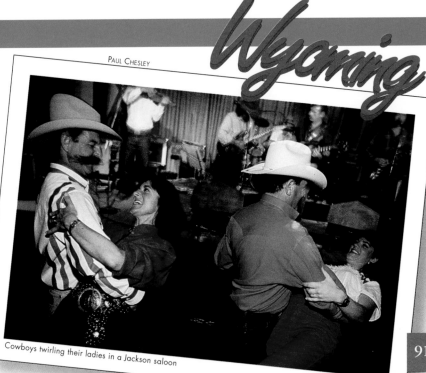

PAUL CHESLEY

Cowboys twirling their ladies in a Jackson saloon

Wyoming's Bighorn Basin. There's a pause in Cody for one of the world's finest Western museums, and another in Thermopolis for some hot springs. Then it's back to the Tetons by way of a high mountain pass carpeted with wildflowers. Throughout the trip, your chances of spotting wildlife are excellent, especially in early summer or autumn. Elk, moose, bison, bighorn sheep, deer, and pronghorn are often seen along these roads.

A true spit-and-dust ranch town at the turn of the century, ❶ **Jackson** ★ *(Jackson Information Center 307-733-3316)* has buffed itself up over the years and today projects a polished New West image in which faded denim competes with iridescent spandex as the fashion fabric of choice. Jackson celebrates its cow-punch heritage with covered boardwalks, Western storefronts, stagecoach rides, chuckwagon dinners, and shoot-outs on the town square. But outfitters here tend to specialize less in saddles than in white-water boats, mountain bikes, skis, and fly-fishing gear. The result is a town that reflects the changing West—a town with a lot to offer.

Start at Jackson's square, with its famous elk antler arches, then poke your head into some of the landmark establishments: the Million Dollar Cowboy Bar, Jackson Drug and its old-time soda fountain, the Wort Hotel and

## Quirky History

Almost every small town in the Rockies has a local history museum. Mannequins in pioneer dress; arrowheads, rifles, knives, and axes; old dentists' drills, rickety wagons, dented trumpets, and mysterious kitchen devices—all crop up again and again, with what some might call mindnumbing regularity.
But usually you'll find at least one startling item to make the stop worthwhile. A two-headed calf, say, or a lamb born with a face on both sides of its head. Or the skull of a miner that still bears the hammer driven into it by irascible Indians. After a while, the quirky charm of these museums lures you in, time after time.

RAYMOND GEHMAN

Bull elk bugling, Yellowstone National Park

its Silver Dollar Bar.

Get a terrific view of the Jackson Hole valley and the mountains surrounding it from either of the two ski areas. The chairlift at **Snow King Ski Resort** *(307-733-5200. Adm. fee)* hoists visitors 1,571 vertical feet and overlooks the town from the south. West of Jackson, the aerial tram at **Jackson Hole Ski Resort** *(Teton Village. 307-733-2291. Adm. fee)* glides past tree line to the summit of Rendezvous Peak—4,139 vertical feet above the valley floor.

The **❷ National Elk Refuge** ★ *(Visitor Center, US 26 N. 307-733-9212)* extends north from the edge of Jackson, encompassing nearly 25,000 acres of rangeland intended to replace the traditional wintering grounds now denied to elk by human settlement. Every year roughly 7,500 elk gather here, and in winter you can get a close look at them from a horse-drawn sleigh. During summer you're unlikely to see any elk, but hawks wheel overhead, waterfowl dabble in the wetlands, and trumpeter swans preen on Flat Creek.

Just north of Jackson on US 26, look for a turreted fieldstone fortress overlooking the valley floor. The building houses the **National Museum of Wildlife Art** ★ *(2820 Rungius Rd. 307-733-5771. Adm. fee)*, an exhibit of paintings, bronzes, and photographs of North American animals rendered by the world's finest wildlife artists. Impressive, moving, and interpreted with intelligence, the works do more than simply depict animals. They also reflect a variety of artistic styles, record phenomena that no longer exist (such as immense bison herds), and present wildlife in compelling western landscapes—from mountains and forests to the high desert.

Continue north a short way and take the right-hand turn for the **Jackson National Fish Hatchery** *(1500 Fish Hatchery Rd. 307-733-2510)*. Here you'll find concrete raceways popu-

lated by dense schools of small, vigorous trout or a few ponderous brood fish. The hatchery, which raises native Snake River cutthroat trout and lake trout, opened in 1957 to boost the populations of fish on the decline from habitat changes, dam construction, and pollution.

Beyond the hatchery, the road climbs a steep embankment. Suddenly, the jagged profile of the **Teton Range** bursts into view. These magnificent peaks, which rise 6,000 to 7,000 feet above the valley floor, form the scenic heart of ❸ **Grand Teton National Park** ★ ★ *(307-739-3600. Adm. fee)*. Deeply glaciated and composed of rock nearly 2.5 billion years old, the Tetons began emerging from the earth's surface just 8 to 10 million years ago. They are the youngest mountains in Wyoming. The park, established in 1929, takes in most of the valley floor and includes several large glacial lakes, a portion of the Snake River, spectacular canyons, and abundant wildlife.

Turn left at Moose Junction to follow Teton Park Road along the base of the mountains. Exhibits at the **Moose Visitor Center** acquaint you with the park's geology, plants, and animals. You can pick up a map at the entrance station. Be sure to make a stop at the **Menor-Noble Historic District** ★, where an old cable ferryboat, buildings, buggies, stagecoaches, and other artifacts recollect the valley's settlement era. It's also a great place to watch the Snake River go by.

93

Miller House, National Elk Refuge, Jackson Hole

No visit to the park would be complete without at least a short hike. The most popular—and crowded—leads 2.4 miles along the southern shore of **Jenny Lake** to Hidden Falls, a lovely waterfall that spills 200 feet from the mouth of Cascade Canyon. Nearby, Inspiration Point overlooks the lake. To avoid the crowds (or at least to find a parking space), start before 10 a.m. You can shorten the hike by taking the boat across the lake. Farther north, another fine trail, accessible from North Jenny Lake Junction, runs beside the sapphire waters of

Snake River and the Teton Range, Jackson Hole

**String Lake,** a popular swimming hole in late summer.

It's easy to miss the turnoff for **Signal Mountain Road ★,** but worthwhile to go back. The incomparable view from the summit takes in nearly the entire length and breadth of the Teton Range, Jackson Lake, and the other mountain ranges that enclose the valley of Jackson Hole.

At Jackson Lake Junction continue north to the **Colter Bay Visitor Center ★,** where you'll find an excellent museum of Native American arts and crafts and a great day hike along the Hermitage Point Trail System.

Say farewell to the Tetons and head for ❹ **Yellowstone National Park ★ ★** *(307-344-7381. Adm. fee)*, keeping an eye out for wildlife. Moose, bison, and elk often turn up among the evergreen forests, sagebrush flats, and broad marshy areas that flank this stretch of road.

Yellowstone, established in 1872 as the world's first national park, sprawls over a landscape of vast forests, intimate meadows, deep canyons, large lakes, waterfalls, rivers, and streams. The park sits atop a geologic hot spot, a place where molten rock rises close enough to the earth's surface to forge restless clusters of geysers, hot springs, fumaroles, and mud pots. These are fascinating geothermal features—strange, marvelous, and reason enough to visit the park. But Yellowstone also embraces a spectacular array of wildlife. There are black bears and grizzlies, bighorn sheep and bison, elk, pronghorn, deer, trumpeter swans, eagles, and many other creatures. What you see depends on when and where you travel.

Just a few miles into the park, the warm waters of Crawfish Creek tumble over a 30-foot cliff, forming **Moose Falls** and a series of pleasant wading pools. Hot springs above the falls warm the water and support crawfish—an unusual animal at this elevation.

Soon you pass into an extensive area of standing dead trees killed by the awesome forest fires that swept through much of Yellowstone during the drought summer of 1988. Spurred on by high winds, the fire that roared through this area easily jumped the 500 yards across **Lewis Canyon** (to your right). Today, tens of thousands of young lodgepole pines thrive on the forest floor. An exhibit at the **Grant Village Visitor Center** explains how fire can benefit Yellowstone's ecosystem.

Small but scenic, the **West Thumb Geyser Basin** ★ lies along a narrow brow of creamy rock overlooking West Thumb, a large bay of Yellowstone Lake. A half-mile boardwalk trail loops down to the lakeshore and circles the hot springs, colorful pools, mud pots, and geysers.

From West Thumb follow the signs for **Lake Village.** The road passes several picnic areas as it hugs the shoreline of **Yellowstone Lake,** the largest mountain lake in North America. At Lake Village you might drop in at the stately **Lake Hotel** ★ *(307-344-7311),* built in the late 1880s and offering fine vistas of the lake and the Absaroka Range.

Turn right at Lake Junction, park, and stroll out onto **Fishing Bridge** ★. Here, in late summer, you can look into the cold, clear water of the Yellowstone River and watch enormous cutthroat trout hold themselves steady in the current and occasionally surface for flies. In early spring the waters jam with spawning trout. Various predators, such as pelicans, eagles, grizzly bears, and ospreys, know about this annual rite and also gather here—for a feast.

Bird watchers may want to stop at the **Fishing Bridge Visitor Center,** where exhibits focus on Yellowstone's birds.

As the road pulls away from the lake, look left for the turnoff to **Lake Butte.** An overlook offers one of the park's finest vistas of Yellowstone Lake and the territory to the southwest, including (on clear days) the Tetons.

---

### More than a Mouthful

For thousands of years, the Plains Indian tribes relied on bison for food, shelter, clothing, and tools. Every part of the animal had a use. The meat—roasted, boiled, or dried—was nourishing and available all year. Brains, liver, kidney, nose gristle, bone marrow, testicles, small intestine—all these were eaten, too, sometimes raw. Some hides were tanned and sewn together for lodge covers; others became warm clothing, storage containers, and shields. Rawhide made fine belts, moccasin soles, bridles, and bow strings. Horns turned into powder flasks, spoons, cups, and ladles. Stirrup covers were often made of bull scrotums, and the phallus—chopped and boiled—would yield a strong glue. Fat could put a fine polish on ceremonial pipes or act as a base for paints, which were often applied with a brush made from the porous bone of a shoulder blade. Ribs made good sled runners, and dried dung substituted for firewood.

## A Volcanic Past

Explosive heat recurs as a theme throughout Yellowstone, and the West Thumb area is no exception. Much of Yellowstone itself is the product of a nearly unimaginable volcanic explosion that blew a hole in the earth's surface measuring 28 miles long by 47 miles across. That calderic explosion happened 600,000 years ago, and the official park map marks its boundaries. Here at West Thumb, a much smaller calderic explosion 150,000 years ago formed the wide, circular crater now occupied by the waters of the bay. Today, intense heat remains so close to the floor of the bay that a large steam explosion could occur here if the lake level drops just a few feet.

A few miles beyond Yellowstone's East Entrance, you'll find **Pahaska Tepee** ★ *(307-527-7701),* a hunting lodge built late in the life of William "Buffalo Bill" Cody. Crowded by a curio shop, restaurant, and dude ranch operation, the two-story log lodge was constructed in 1904 as an elegant, though rustic, retreat for Cody and his high-powered friends. Inside, a wraparound balcony decorated with mounted elk heads overlooks a massive stone hearth and sitting area. Some of the burlwood furnishings, as well as the marble soda fountain, are original to the building.

The road follows the North Fork of the Shoshone River out of the mountains, gradually descending from dense forest to high desert. As the **Shoshone Canyon** opens up, you approach **Buffalo Bill Reservoir,** a broad lake nestled among mountain slopes largely devoid of shade. ❺ **Buffalo Bill State Park** *(307-587-9227)* lies beside the lake, and **Buffalo Bill Dam** ★ impounds its waters. It's worth a stop at the dam's **Interpretive Center** *(307-527-6076)* just to peer over the rim and feel a tingle of vertigo. The gorge is exceptionally narrow, its high walls unusually steep.

Just a short drive from his namesake dam lies Buffalo Bill's namesake town, ❻ **Cody** ★★ *(Chamber of Commerce 307-587-2777).* Founded in 1896, the settlement took Cody's name as a marketing ploy—at the suggestion of the great man himself. A former Pony Express rider, scout, and buffalo hunter who earned a fortune with his Wild West Show, Buffalo Bill became the town's biggest booster and one of its most important investors.

On the western outskirts of Cody, look for **Trail Town** ★ *(1831 DeMaris Dr. 307-587-5302. Mid-May–mid-Sept.; adm. fee),* a double row of weather-beaten pioneer cabins and storefronts moved to the site and stuffed with pioneer

Bison at West Thumb Geyser Basin, Yellowstone National Park

relics. Part ghost town, part pioneer museum, the place includes the grave of Jeremiah Johnston, a trapper made famous by a 1970s Robert Redford film.

Plan to spend more time than expected at the sensational, sprawling **Buffalo Bill Historical Center ★★** *(720 Sheridan Ave. 307-587-4771. Daily May-Oct.; Tues.-Sun. March-April and Nov.; Dec.-Feb. call for hours; adm. fee),* a world-class repository of Western art and Americana divided into four separate museums.

Trail Town, Cody

Start with the **Whitney Gallery of Western Art ★★,** a fabulous collection of original paintings, sculptures, and prints that reflect our ever changing perceptions of the West. Catlin, Miller, Bierstadt, Moran, Bodmer, Rungius, Remington, and Russell—they're all here, along with a couple of the artists' reconstructed studios and some surprises, such as impressionistic landscapes by Remington, an artist too often remembered for cowboy images. The **Cody Firearms Museum ★★** boasts the world's largest collection of American sport and military guns—all in mint condition. The **Plains Indian Museum ★** displays a wealth of arts and crafts, ranging from hide paintings and clothing to weapons and toys. Exhibits examine the origins of the various Plains tribes and explain a bit about their religious beliefs. Finally, there is the **Buffalo Bill Museum ★.** Chock full of glittering saddles, guns, buffalo robes, Wild West Show posters, and family belongings, it tells Cody's story from his youth in Iowa through the show biz days.

Remington's studio, Buffalo Bill Hist. Center

Downtown, stop in at the **Irma Hotel** *(1192 Sheridan Ave. 307-587-4221),* a real beauty built by Buffalo Bill in 1902, named for his daughter, and still putting up guests.

Tucked into the desert foothills, **7 Thermopolis** *(Chamber of Commerce 307-864-3192)* lies along the shaded banks of the Bighorn River, a cool respite for a town best known for its extremely hot water. At **Hot Springs State Park** *(220 Park St. 307-864-2176),* some 3.6 million gallons of crystal-clear, 134°F water flows each day from **Big Springs,** trickling over massive travertine terraces into the river. Soak for free at the **State Bath**

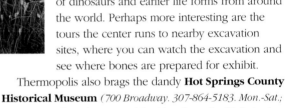

**House** *(307-864-3765)*, or try one of the more extravagant commercial establishments. Then drive the loop roads above the hot springs and look for bison. Or check in at park headquarters or the bathhouse for directions and keys to the petroglyphs at **Legend Rock.**

The **Wyoming Dinosaur Center ★** *(110 Carter Ranch Rd. 307-864-2997 or 800-455-DINO. Adm. fee)* displays full skeletons, skulls, teeth, and other fossilized body parts of a great variety of dinosaurs and earlier life forms from around the world. Perhaps more interesting are the tours the center runs to nearby excavation sites, where you can watch the excavation and see where bones are prepared for exhibit.

Grasses in Wind River Canyon

Thermopolis also brags the dandy **Hot Springs County Historical Museum** *(700 Broadway. 307-864-5183. Mon.-Sat.; adm. fee)*, with a cherrywood backbar from the Hole-in-the-Wall Saloon and an elk hide painting from Chief Washakie.

Heading south, you soon plunge into the **Wind River Canyon ★**, a winding chasm cut through a layer cake of sedimentary rocks by the powerful Wind River. It's a beautiful desert canyon with high, often colorful walls sparsely covered by grass, juniper, and sagebrush. Look for birds and bighorn sheep. A dam blocks the canyon's south end to form **Boysen Reservoir,** a large serpentine lake surrounded by low cliffs, desert hills, and the wide open spaces of the Wind River Basin. ❽ **Boysen State Park** *(307-876-2796)* has campgrounds and picnic areas.

Take US 26 and Wyo. 789 to **Lander,** whose roots go back to the 1860s—about as far as any town in Wyoming. Through the years it has prospered as a center of supply and entertainment for ranchers, miners, oil drillers, and outfitters, as well as the Shoshone and Arapahoe.

Downtown, stop in at the **Fremont County Pioneer Museum ★** *(630 Lincoln St. 307-332-4137. Mon.-Sat.)*. Here among the cases of weird household gadgets, rifles, carpentry tools, branding irons, and other pioneer items, you can gaze upon settler Harvey Morgan's skull, which still bears the hammer driven through it by Indians in 1870.

Southwest of Lander rise the gentle, forested foothills of the Wind River Range. Wyo. 131 climbs into them, following the crystalline Popo Agie River (po-PO-zhuh) into Sinks Canyon, a deep glacial trough. At ❾ **Sinks Canyon State Park ★** *(307-332-3077. Late April–late Oct.,* *depending on snow conditions),* the river careers into the maw of a large limestone cavern and disappears for a quarter mile. It reappears at The Rise, a deep pool often crowded with large trout. Stop at the **Visitor Center** *(Mem. Day–Labor Day)* for a rundown on canyon geology, and keep an eye out for bighorn sheep, deer, and moose.

One of the key landmarks of the Oregon Trail was **⑩ South Pass ★** *(40 miles S of Lander on Wyo. 28).* From an interpretive overlook, gaze across the broad, grassy ramp of the pass and look for ruts left by prairie schooners.

On your way back to Lander, don't miss **South Pass City State Historic Site ★** *(307-332-3682. Mid-May–mid-Oct.),* a restored 1860s gold-mining town. Most of the old buildings are open and furnished, usually with artifacts original to the town. The overall feel is that folks suddenly dropped everything and took off—leaving beer to evaporate in their mugs and the red velvet of the barber's chair to fade in the sunlight. Interpretation is top notch.

Heading northwest from Lander, the next big town is **⑪ Dubois** (DOO-boyce), built along the Wind River where colorful badlands give way to mountain forests. Stop in at the **National Bighorn Sheep Interpretive Center ★** *(907 W. Ramshorn. 307-455-3429. Daily in summer, call for winter hours; adm. fee),* a small but innovative museum that explores the biology and habitat of

Popo Agie River, Sinks Canyon State Park

bighorns and the efforts to reintroduce them to their historical ranges. Next door, the **Dubois Museum** *(307-455-2284. June–mid-Oct.; adm. fee)* focuses on the region's history.

Up the road, the **Tie Hack Memorial** lionizes the lumberjacks who cut hundreds of thousands of railroad ties from these forests until the 1930s. From here, the road climbs over **Togwotee** (TOE-guh-dee) **Pass,** elevation 9,544 feet, and descends back into Jackson Hole with extraordinary vistas of the Teton Range.

# Powder River Region

**200 miles ● 1-2 days ● Late spring through autumn**

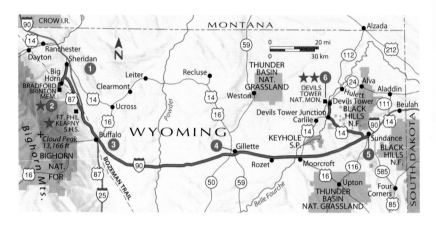

## Johnson County War

A murderous atmosphere permeated northeast Wyoming during the 1880s and '90s, pitting cattle barons against homesteaders and small-time ranchers. Lynchings, shootings, and other foul deeds culminated in the 1892 Johnson County War. A small private army backed by the Wyoming Stockgrowers Association invaded north-central Wyoming. Their object? To kill upward of 20 Johnson County men, including, perhaps, the sheriff, his deputies, and the mayor of Buffalo. Their motive? They accused the men of rustling. Four men died before federal troops defused the confrontation.

Beginning in the foothills of the Bighorn Mountains, this tour follows I-90 east across the vast, lonely grasslands of the Powder River Basin to the forests of the Black Hills. Steeped in history, this region includes some of the bloodiest ground in Wyoming—hotly contested by Indians, settlers, cattle ranchers, and sheepmen. The route visits a couple of battlefields and the site of an important 1860s fort, but sticks mainly to historical houses, downtown areas, and museums before ending on a scenic note—the spectacular geologic oddity of Devils Tower.

Part cow town, part tidy Victorian village, ❶ **Sheridan** *(Chamber of Commerce 307-672-2485)* built up its downtown, now the well-preserved **Main Street Historic District ★**, as a hub for area ranchers, farmers, and coal miners. Start at **King's Saddlery ★** *(184 N. Main St. 307-672-2702 or 800-443-8919)*, an authentic Western landmark that handcrafts custom saddles and lariats, and even brags a Western museum out back. The whiff of leather, rows of cowboy hats, and glimmer of spurs, bits, and belt buckles recall the old days.

For a taste of the high life, visit **Trail End State Historic Site ★** *(Victoria St. and Clarendon Ave. 307-674-4589. Daily July-Aug., p.m. only Sept.–mid-Dec. and April-June; adm. fee)*, an elegant Flemish Revival mansion on expansive grounds overlooking the town. Well preserved and furnished with family belongings, the house was built between 1908 and 1913 for John Kendrick, a cowpoke who came up in the world, ending his days as a three-term U.S. Senator.

Consider winding up your visit with a drink or a meal

at the 1893 **Sheridan Inn** *(5th St. and Broadway. 307-674-5440. Closed Sundays in winter; tour fee)*, a sprawling, rustic hotel with an immense barnlike roof studded by 69 gables. Alas, the gracious old place books no overnight guests.

Hereford bull skull, Bradford Brinton Mem.

South of Big Horn, follow Wyo. 335 to the gleaming white ranch buildings of the ➋ **Bradford Brinton Memorial** ★ *(307-672-3173. Mid-May–Labor Day and by appt.; adm. fee).* Originally an 1890s cattle outfit, the ranch was purchased in 1923 by Bradford Brinton, a wealthy Illinois manufacturer much enamored of the West. He enlarged the neocolonial farmhouse and decorated its rooms with Remingtons, Russells, and other works of Western art. You can visit the house, outbuildings, and an adjacent museum loaded with Native American arts and crafts.

**101**

Evocative and interpreted with intelligence and imagination, **Fort Phil Kearny State Historic Site** ★ *(Visitor Center 307-684-7629. Mid-May–Sept., call for off-season hours; adm. fee)* examines the short, bloody history of the most important Army outpost on the Bozeman Trail. Built in 1866 to protect travelers headed for the Montana goldfields, the fort became a flash point in the struggle between whites and

Little Goose Lodge, Bradford Brinton Memorial

Indians for control of the Powder River region. Not far from its stockaded walls, Capt. William Fetterman and his entire command of 80 soldiers were killed December 21, 1866, in an ambush by Oglala, Arapaho, and Cheyenne warriors. It was the Army's worst defeat at the hands of Plains Indians until Custer met his fate at Little Bighorn in 1876. The Cheyenne burned the fort in 1868, after the Army withdrew.

The **Visitor Center** provides a fine overview of the history and gives a feel for frontier military life. Outside, signs and self-guiding trails mark the locations of various buildings and important landmarks.

Continue south to ❸ **Buffalo** *(Chamber of Commerce 307-684-5544),* an old ranching town tucked into the foothills of the Bighorn Mountains that played a central role in Wyoming's murderous range wars of the 1890s. Many downtown buildings date from that era, but the years have taken their toll on most of the facades. Still, it's worth dropping in at the **Occidental Hotel** *(10 Main St. Tours in summer),* where Owen Wister's hero, the Virginian, got his man. Up the street is the 1884 **Johnson County Courthouse** *(104 Fort St.),* with its graceful double oak staircase and old-timey furniture. Behind the courthouse, you'll find a dainty red sandstone Carnegie library (1909), now housing part of one of the state's better pioneer museums, the **Jim Gatchell Memorial Museum of the West** ★ *(100 Fort St. 307-684-9331. May-Oct. and by appt.; adm. fee).*

Coal lies so close to the surface around ❹ **Gillette** that lightning has been known to ignite the seams and cast a pall of smoke over the area.

Dalby Lake, Gillette

Several of the nation's largest strip mines operate nearby, making Wyoming the country's leading coal producer. Mine tours are sometimes offered in summer; check with the Chamber of Commerce (307-682-3673). The **Campbell County Rockpile Museum** (900 W. 2nd St. 307-682-5723. Closed Sun. Sept.-May) celebrates Gillette's prehistoric and frontier past with stone points and scrapers, cases of antique rifles, old bits and spurs, branding irons, saddles, and wagons.

Outlaw Harry Longabaugh, a.k.a. the Sundance Kid, left his mark throughout the West, but he rarely stayed in one spot very long. In 1887, though, he was compelled to tarry in ❺ **Sundance** (Chamber of Commerce 307-283-1000), sentenced to 18 months in jail for horse theft. At the **Crook County Museum** (309 Cleveland St. 307-283-3666. Mon.-Fri.), you can have a look at his court records and other artifacts.

Finally, detour off I-90 onto US 14 northwest and Wyo. 24 to ❻ **Devils Tower National Monument** ★★ (307-467-5283. Adm. fee), the nation's first national monument, established in 1906. Its centerpiece is a colossal cylinder of bare gray rock that rises, alone, from the gentle, forested landscape of the Black Hills. Oddly scored by hundreds of vertical grooves, this magnificent, flat-topped stump of igneous stone is sacred to Native Americans. It formed underground 60 million years ago from a plume of magma that had pushed upward through layers of soft sedimentary rock. As it cooled, the rock contracted and fractured into a bundle of multisided columns, each measuring about 4 to 8 feet in diameter. For millions of years, the ancestral Belle Fourche (bell FOOSH) River scoured away the surrounding sedimentary rock and exposed the 867-foot tower.

Start your tour at the Visitor Center, then take the half-hour, neck-craning stroll around the base of the tower. Along the way, look for white-tailed deer among the ponderosa pines, and scan the tower for rock climbers.

Devils Tower National Monument

103

### Bear Lodge

Native Americans called Devils Tower Mateo Tepee, or Bear Lodge. The name derives from legends about the tower's formation. Different tribes have slightly different versions, but one story revolves around young girls fleeing from a bear. The bear chases the girls onto the stump of a great tree, where the gods take pity on them and cause the stump to rise toward the heavens. Meanwhile, the enraged bear claws at the sides of the stump until it falls off and dies. In one version the girls become the stars of the Big Dipper. In another they braid a rope from wildflowers and lower themselves back to the ground.

# Wyoming's Old West ★★

535 miles ● 2 to 3 days ● Early summer through autumn ● Snowy Range Road, between Laramie and Saratoga, closes for the winter.

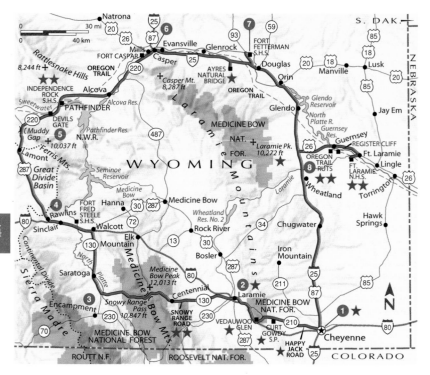

This broad, looping tour of southeastern Wyoming starts in Cheyenne and heads west to climb over high, forested mountains, crossing vast sagebrush flats while stopping to visit both rivers and towns. Mountains of one kind or another rarely drop from view, and there are many chances to spot wildlife—from pronghorn and hawks, to moose, elk, and deer. The route also plunges into history, mainly of the Oregon Trail and the Union Pacific. It also offers hot springs, prisons, and some of the best museums in the state, as well as such landmarks as Independence Rock and the old military outposts along the North Platte River between Casper and Fort Laramie.

Like most towns along Wyoming's southern border, ❶ **Cheyenne** ★ *(Visitors Bureau 307-778-3133 or 800-426-5009)* sprang up during the late 1860s as a rowdy construction camp for the Union Pacific. Today, this serene capital city has a plush, prosperous, downright suburban

Cheyenne Frontier Days Old West Museum

feel to it—a place where you expect to see folks riding lawn mowers rather than horses. Still, Cheyenne has never forgotten it is a Western town, and, as if to prove the point, it throws the country's largest outdoor rodeo bash every July. The heritage is enshrined in Frontier Park at the **Cheyenne Frontier Days Old West Museum** ★ *(4501 Carey Ave. 307-778-7290. Closed Mon. Jan.-April; adm. fee).* A first-rate pioneer museum, it includes Wyoming's finest collection of meticulously restored horse-drawn carriages and wagons.

105

Money poured into Cheyenne during the cattle boom and gold rush years of the 1870s and '80s. Cattle barons, bankers, and merchants built impressive mansions, now mostly demolished, as well as stately churches and commercial buildings. Many survive downtown on Capitol Avenue between the spectacular **Union Pacific Depot** and the **State Capitol** *(Capitol Ave. and 24th St. 307-777-7220. Mon.-Fri.).* Nearby, you can walk through the **Historic Governors' Mansion** *(300 E. 21st St. 307-777-7878. Tues.-Sat.),* an elegant colonial revival house with a few cowpoke touches.

From Cheyenne, follow Wyo. 210 toward the gentle crest of the Laramie Mountains. Known to the locals as **Happy Jack Road** ★, this worthwhile drive leaves most travelers feeling a bit smug and superior for having shunned the interstate. It passes **Curt Gowdy State Park** ★ *(307-632-7946. Adm. fee),* then climbs into open pine forests and rolling grass meadows studded with weathered formations of granite 1.4 billion years old. Forest Road 700 leads to some of the best formations, in **Vedauwoo** (VEE-duh-voo) **Glen** ★. From there, you can pick up I-80 to Laramie.

State Capitol, Cheyenne

Today it's a placid university town, but early on
**② Laramie ★** *(Chamber of Commerce 307-745-7339)* was a
classic hell-on-wheels railroad town—so wild, so corrupt, so
eye-gouging mean it was put under the jurisdiction of federal courts until 1874. Was it ironic or merely convenient that
the territory's first prison was built here? Used from 1872 to

Weathered granite formations, Vedauwoo Glen

1901, the **Wyoming
Territorial Prison ★**
has been restored
well beyond its
1890s condition and
is today the center-
piece of the
**Wyoming Territor-
ial Park ★** *(975
Snowy Range Rd. 307-
745-6161. Daily mid-
May–Sept., call for
off-season hours; adm.
fee for museums).* Spot-
less, bright, stuffed
with excellent
exhibits, the prison
offers guided and self-guided tours through the cellblocks,
dining hall, warden's office, and infirmary. The park also
includes the **National U.S. Marshals Museum ★,** a frontier
town reproduction, with actors in period costume.

Elsewhere in town, the **Laramie Plains Museum ★**
*(603 Ivinson Ave. 307-742-4448. Feb.-Dec. Mon.-Sat.; adm. fee)*
displays its fine collection of pioneer memorabilia at the
stone-and-shingle, Queen Anne-style **Ivinson Mansion.**

On the University of Wyoming campus, check out the
**American Heritage Center ★** *(2111 Willett Dr. 307-766-4114.
Mon.-Fri.),* a large conical building with such diverse items as
Jack Benny's fiddle and Alfred Jacob Miller's oil painting of
the 1834 Rendezvous, which he attended. Next door, the
**University of Wyoming Art Museum** *(307-766-6622. Feb.-
Dec. Tues.-Sun.; adm. fee)* displays works by Moran and Rus-
sell as well as Andy Warhol and Robert Rauschenberg. The
fine **Geology Museum** *(307-766-4218)* has one of the
world's few mounted skeletons of an Apatosouras.

From Laramie, head west on Wyo. 130, also called
**Snowy Range Road ★ ★.** One of the most scenic drives in
the Rockies, it climbs through dense forests onto the broad

back of the Medicine Bow Mountains, bowling along at roughly 10,000 feet through vast fields of wildflowers in late spring and summer. On clear days you can see as far south as Rocky Mountain National Park in Colorado.

On the west side of the mountains, consider a short side trip south on Wyo. 230 to ❸ **Encampment,** where the **Grand Encampment Museum** ★ *(7th and Barnett Sts. 307-327-5308. Mem. Day–Labor Day; call for off-season hours)* preserves a ghost town of buildings plus artifacts from an 1890s copper boom.

If you feel like soaking in a hot springs, follow the signs in **Saratoga** *(Chamber of Commerce 307-326-8855)* to **Saratoga Hot Springs** ★, a big pool and bathhouse on the North Platte River. The town also offers good meals and lodging in a historical setting at the 1890s **Wolf Hotel** ★ *(101 E. Bridge St. 307-326-5525)*, and culture at the **Saratoga Museum** *(104 Constitution Ave. 307-326-5511. Mem. Day–Labor Day; adm. fee)*.

Several stone chimneys stand at attention beside the North Platte River at **Fort Fred Steele State Historic Site** *(9 miles E of Sinclair. 307-320-3013. May–mid-Sept.)*. Built along the Union Pacific route in 1868 to protect railroad construction workers, little remains except foundations, a stone powder house, and a rock corral.

Founded in 1868 as a railroad town, ❹ **Rawlins** *(Chamber of Commerce, 519 W. Cedar St. 307-324-4111. Walking tour map available)* prospered early as a supply point for the gold rush towns of Atlantic City and South Pass City. Later, it got in on the livestock boom. By the turn of the century, its well-to-do were building impressive Victorian houses and fancy commercial buildings. Several survive, including the 1903 **Ferris Hotel** *(Seasonal bed and breakfast. 607 W. Maple St. 307-324-3961)* and the forlorn **Union Pacific Depot.**

Pillows made from prison uniforms, Wyoming Frontier Prison, Rawlins

Tour guides, well versed in the lore of rioting inmates drunk on Vitalis, lead tours of the **Wyoming Frontier Prison** ★ *(5th and Walnut Sts. 307-324-4422. Mid-May–Sept. and by appt.; adm. fee)*. In service from 1901 to 1981, this old fortress is much gloomier and truer to prison life than Laramie's spick-and-span territorial prison.

Two of the Oregon Trail's most notable landmarks—Devils Gate and Independence Rock—lie almost within sight of one another along Wyo. 220. At ❺ **Devils Gate** the Sweetwater River rushes through a narrow gorge 370 feet deep and as little as 50 feet wide. Emigrants often camped here and explored the gorge. Some wrote of wading through the passage, others of scaling the bluffs and peering into the gorge. A few are said to have fallen in.

Named by fur trappers celebrating the Fourth of July, **Independence Rock** ★★ rises from the windswept prairie as an immense oblong hump. Some emigrants described it as a great beached whale, others as the back of a huge turtle. Thousands clambered over it during the

Devils Gate

covered wagon years and chiseled their names into the granite surface—often with gravestone precision. A trail loops around the base of the rock, and you can still scramble to its rounded summit, where the view has changed little since before the 1860s.

Continue northeast along Wyo. 220 to ❻ **Casper** *(Chamber of Commerce 307-234-5311),* a city with roots that run deeper than its modern office buildings and industrial sprawl suggest. It lies along the banks of the North Platte River, with the Laramie Mountains rising as a dark, abrupt wall to the south.

Most recently a center for gas and oil production, Casper traces its history to the mid-19th century, when thousands of Oregon Trail emigrants crossed the North Platte more or less where I-25 breezes over the water

Independence Rock

today. Ferry services and toll bridges operated in the area during the 1840s and '50s. In 1859 the Army assigned a cavalry troop to what was then called Platte Bridge Station. After an 1865 fight with Plains Indians left Lt. Caspar Collins and 26 others dead, the place was renamed Fort Caspar.

The outpost was reconstructed in the 1930s as the **Fort Caspar Museum** ★ *(4001 Fort Caspar Rd. 307-235-8462. Daily mid-May–mid-Sept., museum closed Sat. mid-Sept.–mid-May).* Its log buildings, furnished in period style, depict military and emigrant life along the Oregon Trail. An adjacent museum features exhibits on central Wyoming history.

Housed in a renovated power plant, the **Nicolaysen Art Museum** *(400 E. Collins Dr. 307-235-5247. Tues.-Sun.; adm. fee)* includes a Discovery Center where children can putter with watercolors while parents wander among art of the region and the world.

A graceful arch of limestone in a natural amphitheater of smooth, red sandstone, **Ayres Natural Bridge** ★ *(County Road 13 S to Natural Bridge Park. 307-358-3532. Adm. fee)* protrudes from a high bluff and spans the clear waters of La Prele Creek. There are few better places in this hot, thirsty country for a picnic. Here, box elders, chokecherries, and poplars shade the creek and picnic grounds and clouds of cliff swallows dart overhead.

It's worth stopping at
**❼ Fort Fetterman State Historic Site** *(10 miles NW of Douglas on Wyo. 93. 307-358-2864. Mem. Day–Labor Day)* just for the compelling, lonesome view. Built on a windy, unshaded plateau, the fort, a hardship post, overlooks the North Platte River and the swelling plains of central Wyoming. Two 1870s buildings survive. One serves as a

## Beloved Horse Thief

Top hand, rowdy card player, and horse thief of a thousand alibis, George Pike was Douglas's most famous cowboy. Though he stole, his neighbors liked him for his quick wit, sense of fair play, and downright shamelessness. When Pike died in 1908, his last employer erected an expensive tombstone with the following inscription:

Underneath this stone in eternal rest

Sleeps the wildest one of the wayward West.

He was underneath a gambler and sport and cowboy, too,

And he led the pace in an outlaw crew.

He was sure on the trigger and staid to the end

But was never known to quit on a friend.

In the relations of death all mankind's alike

But in life there was only one George W. Pike.

109

Ayres Natural Bridge spanning La Prele Creek

museum exhibiting the trappings of military life, some homesteading gear, a fine map of Wyoming's emigrant trails, and other good stuff.

Home of the **Wyoming State Fair,** held each year in August, **Douglas** (*Chamber of Commerce 307-358-2950*) is an old cow town laid out along the shady banks of the North Platte River. During the 1880s it boasted 25 saloons, each specializing in the lubrication of hard-working cowboys. A massive backbar from one of those saloons stands in the **Wyoming Pioneer Memorial Museum ★** (*400 W. Center St. 307-358-9288. Mem. Day–Sept. Mon.-Fri.*), along with an impressive collection of Native American arts and crafts; a saddle owned by range detective Tom Horn; loads of guns; and dulcimers, fiddles, and mandolins used to beat back the lonely winter shadows of the wind-raked plains.

At many trail-rut sites along the Oregon Trail, it's sometimes hard to distinguish bona fide wagon ruts from jeep trails. But there can be no mistaking the **❽ Oregon Trail Ruts ★ ★** left in the hills south of **Guernsey.** There, a topographical bottleneck forced emigrants to drive their wagons over a grassy ridge of sandstone. The wheels eventually carved ruts as deep as 5 feet. From the well-marked parking area, a short trail climbs to these vivid, trenchlike ruts.

Costumed guide, Sutler Store, Fort Laramie National Historic Site

Many of those who helped cut the ruts camped the previous night a few miles downriver at **Register Cliff** (*Follow the signs*), where they carved their names into the 60-foot bluff of tan sandstone. Visible names date back to the 1840s and '50s. Many are now protected by a chain-link fence—an unfortunate necessity brought on by legions of modern vandals.

One of the finest living history museums in the West, **Fort Laramie National Historic Site ★ ★** (*3 miles S of Fort Laramie on Wyo. 160. 307-837-2221. Adm. fee*) preserves a dozen restored military buildings and portrays the lives of garrisoned soldiers, their wives, and hangers-on.

Built in 1834 as a fur-trading post near the confluence

Cavalry Barracks, Fort Laramie N.H.S.

of the Laramie and North Platte Rivers, Fort Laramie later became one of the most important stopovers on the Oregon Trail and a major military outpost. With a third of their 2,000-mile journey to Oregon complete, emigrants stopped here to rest, repair their wagons, and gape at a semipermanent encampment of Lakota. Pony Express riders passed through here. Later, so did stagecoaches running between Cheyenne and Deadwood. Two important treaties—in 1851 and 1868—with the Plains tribes were signed here, and the Army used the fort as a staging area for campaigns once those treaties failed.

Restored buildings include barracks, officers quarters, guardhouses, a stone magazine, the post trader's store, and a few rather elegant houses for the highest ranking officers. These have been completely furnished with great care, intelligence, and accuracy from a treasure trove of period artifacts. In the cavalry barracks, for instance, stretch row upon row of bunks, each with a straw mattress, a wool blanket, and a couple of pegs on the wall where canteens dangle among uniforms.

The grounds, buildings, and excellent Visitor Center museum are open all year, but the best time to visit is from early June to mid-August, when the living history program is going full tilt. That's when you can flag down a soldier and ask him about his breech-loading rifle, or cut a deal for a twist of tobacco with the post trader, or buy a round for the recruits playing cards at the enlisted men's bar.

## Mormon Handcart Disaster

Between 1843 and 1868, roughly 400,000 people crossed central Wyoming on the Oregon Trail. Most freighted their belongings in covered wagons, but approximately 3,000 Mormons who could not afford wagons walked to the Salt Lake Valley pulling handcarts. Though most arrived in Utah with little trouble, two handcart groups, with an average of 500 people each, met with disaster in 1856 when an October blizzard swept through central Wyoming. Short on rations and unprepared for subzero weather, the Mormons lost roughly 200 people to starvation and exposure before relief wagons from Salt Lake got them to Utah.

# Along the Green River ★

**400 miles ● 2 to 3 days ● Early summer through autumn**

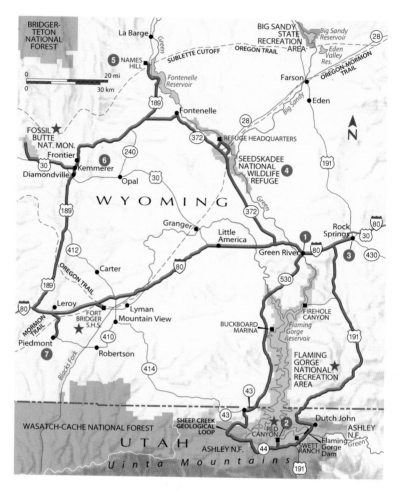

As it meanders through the high desert lands and towns of southwestern Wyoming, this route dips into most of the important eras of Rocky Mountain history and pre-history—ancient fossils, the fur trade, the Oregon Trail, and the construction of the transcontinental railroad. The scenery, though occasionally spectacular, consists mainly of the rolling sagebrush hills and plains along the Green River.

The drive starts in the railroad town of ❶ **Green River** *(Chamber of Commerce 307-875-5711).* Founded in 1868 as a watering hole for the Union Pacific Railroad, it lies among desert hills capped by low cliffs and a few jutting rock spires. Before the rails arrived, emigrants heading for Utah, California, and Oregon passed this way, as did the overland stage. Today, the town's economy owes much to the mining and processing of trona, a rare but unglamorous mineral with a multitude of uses.

For a quick rundown on the area's history, stop at the **Sweetwater County Museum** *(In the courthouse, 80 W. Flaming Gorge Way. 307-872-6435. Sept.-June Mon.-Fri., July-Aug. Mon.-Sat.)*. But to actually plant your feet where history was made, follow the signs to **Expedition Island National Historic Landmark** *(South 2nd E)*. From there, in 1869, the explorer John Wesley Powell ventured with nine men in four small boats into the great unknown—a thousand-mile journey down the Green and Colorado Rivers. On this and subsequent expeditions, Powell mapped much of the canyon country of the Southwest. A series of plaques planted among the island's picnic tables record the exploits of others who braved the white water.

From Green River, follow Wyo. 530 south into the sprawling high desert lands around **Flaming Gorge National Recreation Area** ★ *(Ashley National Forest 801-784-3445)*. Once roaring with white water, the Green River was dammed in the early 1960s, creating a 91-mile-long lake that extends from Utah into Wyoming. This usually placid serpentine body of water winds through a variety of landscapes: open sagebrush-covered hills, narrow side canyons, and, of course, the great precipitous void of Flaming Gorge itself, where vivid red walls sometimes rise nearly 1,500 feet above the waters.

Flaming Gorge National Recreation Area

The most rewarding section of this 146-mile drive from Green River to Rock Springs starts south of Manila, Utah, on Utah 44. A side road, the **Sheep Creek Geological Loop,** cuts through tilted layers of sedimentary stone along the Uinta Mountains and offers a good chance to see bighorn sheep. Nearby, you can visit **Ute Tower,** a 1930s fire lookout with a panoramic vista of Flaming Gorge and the Uintas.

Farther along Utah 44, take the turnoff to **②** **Red Canyon Visitor Center ★**, which overlooks one of the most spectacular sections of the gorge and offers an overview of the area's animals, geology, and history. You can also wander among the modest cabins and outbuildings of a 1909 homestead, **Swett Ranch Historic Site** *(0.5 mile N of US 191 junction on FR 158. Mem. Day–Labor Day).* Heading north on US 191, stop at **Flaming Gorge Dam** and view the Green River flowing far below, with some of the best trout waters in the West. The Visitor Center here offers tours of the power plant.

Continue north to I-80 for windblown, dusty, tough **③** **Rock Springs** *(Chamber of Commerce, 1897 Dewar Dr. 307-362-3771. Mon.-Fri. Walking tour brochures available),* which boomed as a coal-mining town after the Union Pacific arrived in 1868. Its miners still dig coal, as well as trona. Rich in history both uplifting and disreputable, the city once boasted more than 50 different nationalities. Folks didn't always get along. In 1885 a white mob descended on Chinatown and killed 28 people. Near the railroad tracks downtown, you'll find some attractive old buildings, including **City Hall,** a grand stone fortress that houses the **Rock Springs Museum** *(201 B St. 307-362-3138. Tues.-Sat. in summer, Wed.-Sat. off-season).*

Returning to Green River along I-80, drive northwest on Wyo. 372, out on the great sagebrush plains west of the Wind River Range. Here **④** **Seedskadee National Wildlife Refuge** *(307-875-2187)* hugs the banks of the Green River for more than 35 miles. It takes its name from a Shoshone word meaning "river of the prairie hen" (sage grouse), and it provides crucial habitat for more than 200 bird species, as well as moose, deer, pronghorn, and other wildlife. The river—broad and swift—curves through the arid land like a sinuous oasis, supporting groves of cottonwoods, willow thickets, and marshy areas. Stop at headquarters for a map, then follow the wildlife drive along the benchlands. Besides sage grouse, you're likely to see Canada geese, pintails, mallards, sandhill cranes, great blue herons, and various birds of prey. Trumpeter swans winter at Dodge Bottom. Most of the refuge is open for hiking.

Continue northward to **⑤** **Names Hill** *(S of LaBarge on US 189),* a low limestone cliff where travelers on the Oregon Trail paused to etch their names after making one of the trip's most dangerous river crossings. Names include

## Repent While Sinning

One of Kemmerer's early saloon keepers, Preaching Lime Huggins, hung signs in his place reminding thirsty miners to make sure their kids had enough food and clothing before they bellied up to his bar. One customer reportedly said he preferred bending the elbow at Huggins' place because he could "repent while sinning and get the whole thing over at once."

114

Jim Bridger's (behind the fence), but many doubt that the great mountain man, an illiterate, carved the letters himself. Sadly, names added during the past 30 years nearly obliterate many carved 140 years ago. It's outrageous that any modern traveler—conveyed here by a mere foot on the gas pedal—would believe his presence somehow ranks with that of people who arrived after 1,500 miles on a buckboard.

To the south on US 189, another old mining town, **6** **Kemmerer** *(Chamber of Commerce 307-877-9761)*, has been hauling coal from the ground since 1897. Remembered as a hard-drinking as well as a hard-working town, Kemmerer celebrates its liquor lore at the **Fossil Country Museum** *(400 Pine Ave. 307-877-6551. Mon.-Sat.)*. There, among the usual pioneer relics, you'll find a proud display of copper moonshine stills ranging in size from stove top to near industrial. All bubbled merrily during Prohibition.

Kemmerer is also the proud home of J.C. Penney, founder of the chain of department stores. Penney's first store, the Golden Rule, opened here in 1902 but no longer stands. You can visit the restored **J.C. Penney House** *(307-877-3164. Mid-May–mid-Sept.; off-season, stop at the Penney's store down the street)*, a modest clapboard home

115

Storm along US 189 near Names Hill

where Penney lived during the early years of his fairy-tale rise to wealth.

One of the world's great fossil repositories, **Fossil Butte National Monument** ★ *(14 miles W of Kemmerer on US 30. 307-877-4455)* preserves a portion of an ancient lake bed where the remains of a remarkable number of fish, reptiles, birds, mammals, and plants have lain for 50 million years. Renowned not only for the sheer number of fossils but also for their great variety and amazing detail, Fossil Butte gives one of the clearest views we have of an Eocene ecosystem.

The ancient freshwater lake—glimmering at the foot of mountains long gone—teemed with at least 20 different species of fish, including big gars and great schools of fish similar to modern herring. Turtles and crocodiles wallowed in the muck, and small horses, early primates, snakes, and birds lived among a lush shoreline forest of palms, figs, and cypresses. Willows, beeches, oaks, and maples stood among the foothills, and a spruce-fir forest grew on the cool mountainsides.

The flattened remains of these and many other plants and animals now lie between thin layers of stone, like flowers pressed between the pages of a book. At the **Visitor Center** you'll find dark, rock-hard fossils embedded in small platters and great slabs of pale sedimentary rock. Fish retain entire skeletons, teeth, scales, even skin.

Piedmont ghost town

There's an immense crocodile, an entire school of fish, a stingray, the delicate bones of a bat, and the leaves, stems, and flowers of various plants. Exhibits and interpretive trails explain how fossils were formed, discovered, and prepared. You can dig your own fossils at nearby commercial quarries *($35 to $55 a day)* or buy them. **Ulrich's Fossil Gallery** *(Near the monument entrance)* is worth the stop just to browse.

Head south back to I-80 and the beautiful, marked drive to the railroad ghost town of ❼ **Piedmont** *(Leroy exit from I-*

*80, then southward on dirt roads. Obey posted areas).* You can poke around in three beehive-shaped kilns built in 1869 to supply charcoal for smelters near Salt Lake and fuel for trains. Piedmont is also the site of an unusually well-timed labor uprising. In May 1869 Union Pacific Vice President Thomas Durant rolled into town, eager to reach Promontory, Utah, for the transcontinental

Charcoal kilns, Piedmont

railroad's last spike festivities. Angry workers, unpaid for five months, surrounded his palace car and refused to let it move until he paid up. Durant wired for the half million and went on his way.

Back on I-80 is the site of what was originally a trading post built in 1843 by mountain man Jim Bridger. **Fort Bridger,** however, carved a more lasting niche in history as a frontier military outpost. Today, its restored buildings, along with a first-rate replica of Bridger's original mud-and-log trading post, comprise **Fort Bridger State Historic Site ★** *(307-782-3842. Daily May-Oct., Sat.-Sun. March-April and Oct.-Nov.; adm. fee).*

Bridger and his partner, Louis Vasquez, built their trading post mainly to supply emigrants heading west along the Oregon Trail, among them Brigham Young and a growing number of his Mormon followers. At first cordial, Bridger and Young eventually fought for control of both the trading post and the lucrative ferry crossings on the Green River. The Mormons built a rival post, Fort Supply, in 1853, attempted to buy Fort Bridger in 1855, and burned both to the ground in 1857 as federal troops advanced on Salt Lake during the Utah War. The Army rebuilt and expanded the fort, occupying it on and off until 1890.

The remaining buildings, dating from the late 1850s, are furnished in period style and are sometimes occupied by a costumed guide. The fort's museum, housed in an 1888 barracks, exhibits military equipment and fur trade artifacts.

The site also hosts the **Fort Bridger Annual Mountain Man Rendezvous ★** *(Labor Day weekend),* when thousands of modern-day buckskinners—history buffs, really—come dressed in pre-1840s garb, intent on re-creating the glorious hullabaloo of a Rocky Mountain fur-trapping rendezvous.

**117**

### Glorious Outrage

If you lived in the Rockies during the 1820s and '30s, you spent most of the year wading ice-cold streams, roasting bison ribs, living with and learning from Indians, and building up a nice bundle of beaver pelts. Come summer, you headed for a pre-arranged site—Wyoming's Green River Valley, more often than not—for the annual rendezvous. There, you might trade your furs for supplies, equipment, trinkets, and whiskey, all of which had arrived by caravan from St. Louis.

Much more than just a business convention, the rendezvous was the social highlight of the year—a drunk and disorderly, bawdy, and thoroughly outrageous good time when trappers gambled, fought, raced their horses, bragged, and caught up on the news.

# Denver-Mountain Loop ★★

## 225 miles ● 3 to 4 days ● Summer through autumn. Trail Ridge Road closed in winter

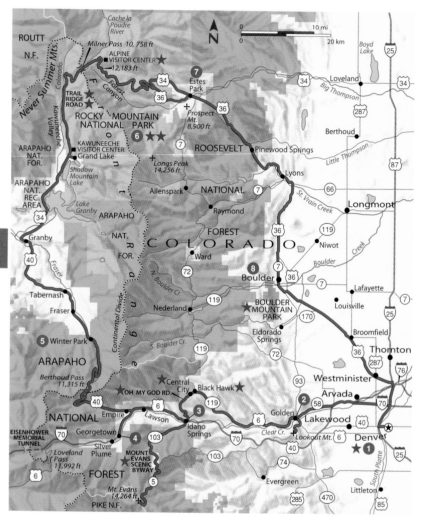

Starting on the floor of the Great Plains and climbing high above tree line in the Rocky Mountains, this spectacular loop through north-central Colorado takes in jaw-dropping scenery and repeatedly recalls the late 19th century, when the mountains west of Denver teemed with miners. Few drives in the Rockies gather so much of the West into one strand. Its art, history, cultures, natural wonders, and pleasant diversions are all well represented.

From Denver the route heads west to Golden, where

you can knock back free beer and sake, poke around the best railroad museum in the Rockies, and drive to Buffalo Bill's grave, which overlooks the plains and mountains. Next comes a procession of tidy Victorian mining towns: Central City, with its bustling casinos; Idaho Springs, with its underground mine tours; and Georgetown, with its looping steam train ride. Then it's north to Winter Park for some mountain biking, and on to Rocky Mountain National Park, renowned for its top-of-the-world vistas, expansive alpine tundra, and varied wildlife. Finally, the route winds back down to the plains through Estes Park and Boulder.

One of the region's few major urban areas, ❶ **Denver** ★ *(Visitors Bureau 303-892-1112)* sprawls west of the Great Plains, facing the long, imposing wall of the Rockies. Some travelers, lured by the high country and put off by the crush of traffic, hurry away from Denver—and miss a lot. Even a quick run through the city's top-notch museums will send you on your way with a much better understanding of Colorado and, indeed, the entire Rocky Mountain West.

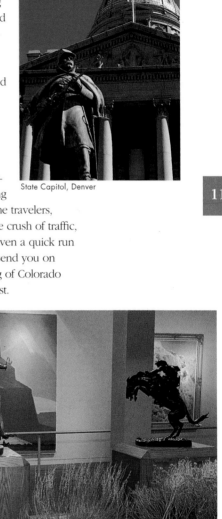

State Capitol, Denver

119

Sculptures by Charles M. Russell and Frederic Remington in the Museum of Western Art, Denver

Start downtown beneath the gold-leaf dome of the **Colorado State Capitol** *(200 E. Colfax. 303-866-2604. Tours Mon.-Fri.),* then head for the **Colorado History Museum** ★ ★ *(1300 Broadway. 303-866-3682. Adm. fee),* which offers a good overview of the region's Indians, fur trappers, miners, cowboys, sodbusters, and other characters. Nearby, fabulous galleries at the **Denver Art Museum** ★ *(100 W. 14th Ave. Pkwy. 303-640-2793. Tues.-Sun.; adm. fee except Sat.)* display Native American art from pre-Columbian times forward. A few blocks away, the redbrick **Museum of Western Art** ★ *(1727 Tremont Pl. 303-296-1880. Tues.-Sat.; adm. fee)* shows the West through the works of Remington, Russell, Bierstadt, Moran, and O'Keeffe, displayed in this turn-of-the-century bordello.

Watch coins sweep through the works of the **U.S. Mint** ★ *(320 W. Colfax Ave. 303-844-3582. Mon.-Fri.),* or tour the **Denver Firefighters Museum** *(1326 Tremont Pl. 303-892-1436. Mon.-Fri.; adm. fee),* outfitted with old uniforms, carts, and fire trucks.

On the west side of the South Platte River, dawdle among rare antique autos, buggies, railroad cars, and airplanes at the **Forney Transportation Museum** *(1416 Platte. 303-433-3643. Adm. fee).* Next door, the **Platte Valley Trolley,** a 1920s replica, will take you to the **Children's Museum of Denver** ★ *(303-433-7444. Tues.-Sun.; adm.*

Enjoying the kid's slide at the Children's Museum of Denver

*fee),* where kids can ski all year on artificial snow, explore the science lab, and blow hot and cold in the weather studio.

East of downtown, get a preview of Rocky Mountain wildlife at the **Denver Zoo** ★ *(E. 23rd and Steele Sts. 303-331-4110. Adm. fee),* one of the nation's finest all-around zoos, with imaginative exhibits of exotic animals from all over the world. Nearby, offerings at the massive **Denver Museum of Natural History** ★ ★ *(2001 Colorado Blvd. 303-322-7009. Adm. fee)* include a planetarium, an IMAX movie theater, and a highly acclaimed walk-through tutorial on the evolution of life with fossils, reconstructed

ancient habitats, and full dinosaur skeletons and models.

Elsewhere, stroll the rose, herb, rock, and Japanese gardens at the **Denver Botanic Gardens** ★ *(1005 York St. 303-331-4000. Adm. fee),* and learn about African-American miners and cowboys at the **Black American West Museum and Heritage Center** *(3091 California. 303-292-2566. Adm. fee).*

Freight car lock, Colorado Railroad Museum

From Denver, head west on I-70 and take Colo. 58 into Clear Creek Canyon. On the outskirts of ❷ **Golden** *(Chamber of Commerce 303-279-3113),* stop at the **Colorado Railroad Museum** ★ *(17155 W. 44th Ave. 303-279-4591. Adm. fee)* and hoist yourself aboard the old locomotives that once plied Colorado's mountains, canyons, and plains. Inside, you'll find a huge model train layout, miniature steam locomotives that ran at amusement parks, and cases of memorabilia.

The train museum lies within sniffing distance of the malty **Coors Brewing Company** *(12th and Ford Sts. 303-277-BEER. Mon.-Sat.).* Most visitors seem to regard the tour through this mammoth industrial brewing complex as a necessary preliminary to the main event—quaffing free beer. Nearby, sip another traditional drink—sake—and learn how it is brewed at **Hakushika Sake U.S.A. Corporation** *(4414 Table Mountain Dr. 303-279-SAKE. Mon.-Fri.; tours by reservation).*

For a smashing view of the Great Plains, Denver, and the spine of Colorado's Front Range, drive to the Lookout Mountain summit and visit **Buffalo Bill's Grave and Museum** *(987 ½ Lookout Mt. Rd. 303-526-0747. Tues.-Sun.; adm. fee).* The museum reviews William Cody's life as a Pony Express rider, hunter, scout, and—above all—a showman. His grave is notable for the abundance of small change strewn over it. After all these years, folks are still throwing money at old Bill.

Hibiscus, Denver Botanic Gardens

Follow US 6 west from Golden through Clear Creek Canyon, then north on Colo. 119 to the historic mining—now booming casino—towns of **Black Hawk** ★ and **Central City** ★ *(For both contact Gilpin Chamber of Commerce 303-582-5077).* A gold strike in 1859 kicked off a mining boom that lasted some 40 years and paid for the fancy Victorians that still line the streets. Most of the old buildings now house casinos jammed with glittering, beeping slot machines, card tables, and bars.

Begin at Central City's 1872 **Teller House** ★ *(120 Eureka St. 303-582-3200)*, a fine old hotel where President Ulysses S. Grant is said to have passed out in 1873 and where entertainers from Sarah Bernhardt to Mae West have spent the night. Guided tours of the hotel's splendid upper rooms include spirited anecdotes about the town and its peculiar characters.

Fringed jacket, Buffalo Bill's Grave and Museum

Next door stands the 1878 **Central City Opera House** ★ *(200 Eureka St. 303-292-6700. Tours from the Teller House; adm. fee)*, kept cool by 4-foot walls of stone and a creek running under the floorboards. Mark Twain got a few laughs here, actor Edwin Booth declaimed, and a top-notch opera company still performs during the summer.

Another worthwhile stop is the **Gilpin County Historical Society Museum** *(228 E. High St. 303-582-5283. Mem. Day–Labor Day; adm. fee)*, an extensive "county attic museum" housed in an enormous 1870 schoolhouse and stuffed with early mining artifacts and such oddball items as a church pew that converts into a pool table.

From Central City you can follow **Oh My God Road** ★ *(Closed in winter, check with locals for driving conditions)* over the mountains and down tortuous Virginia Canyon to Idaho Springs. This gravel backcountry route is dotted with old shaft houses and mine entrances, and it offers terrific views to the south of 14,264-foot Mount Evans. **Mount Evans Scenic Byway** ★, the highest passenger car road in the world, climbs within 130 feet of the summit. You can pick up the highway in Idaho Springs.

Another mining town that sprang up during the 1860s and prospered as both a gold- and silver-mining district, ❸ **Idaho Springs** is today a tourist stop with a mother lode of mine tours. The most obvious of the bunch is the big red **Argo Gold Mill** *(2350 Riverside Dr. 303-567-2421. Adm. fee)*, where guides rattle off the story of this historical stamp mill at auctioneer velocity. A better bet is the **Edgar Experimental Mine** *(365 8th Ave. 303-567-2911. Tues.-Sat.; adm. fee)*, where the Colorado School of Mines conducts tours through the underground workings. Duck into the small, family-owned **Phoenix Gold Mine** *(Stanley Rd., then W 1 mile to Trail Creek Rd. 303-567-0422. Adm. fee)*, and you might hear miners drilling or blasting while you learn about drifts, shafts, pillars, and muck plates.

Several miles up the canyon is ❹ **Georgetown,** another prosperous Victorian mining town jammed with turn-of-the-century houses and commercial buildings. Two of the finest are open for tours: the 1867 **Hamill House** *(305 Argentine St. 303-569-2840. Daily June-Sept., Sat.-Sun. Oct.-May; adm. fee)* and the 1875 **Hotel de Paris** *(409 6th St. 303-569-2311. Daily June-Sept., Sat.-Sun. Oct.-May; adm. fee).*

The town's biggest draw, though, is the **Georgetown Loop Railroad** ★ *(1106 Rose Street. 303-569-2403 or 800-691-4FUN. Daily Mem. Day–Sept., call for winter schedule; adm. fee),* a narrow gauge steam train that chuffs and clangs over a winding course between Georgetown and Silver Plume. An 1880s engineering marvel, the railroad crosses four bridges, makes exceedingly tight curves, and actually spirals over itself at the famous Loop—all in order to gain 638 feet while maintaining a maximum 4 percent grade. It's a fine, lurching ride, with black smoke wafting back over the open cars, clouds of steam occasionally thundering from the flanks of the locomotive, and the hoarse chord of the whistle echoing through the canyon. As part of the trip, you can get an underground tour of the **Lebanon Silver Mine.**

123

From Georgetown, double back on I-70 and take US 40 northwest over Berthoud Pass (11,315 feet) to ❺ **Winter Park** *(Chamber of Commerce 970-726-4118)* and the **Fraser River Valley.** Surrounded by forests and broad, 12,000-foot peaks, this valley is laced with over 500 miles of excellent mountain-biking

Georgetown Loop Railroad steam locomotive

trails. Some climb high along tumbling mountain streams; others meander easily along the valley floor.

Or avoid the climb entirely by riding the **Zephyr Chairlift** ★ *(Adm. fee)* at **Winter Park Resort** *(677 Winter Park Drive. 970-726-5514).* The chairlift boosts bike riders and hikers nearly 2,000 vertical feet and opens up 45 miles of trails through forest and meadow. Or you can ride down the slopes on a half-mile **Alpine Slide** ★ *(Adm. fee).*

Continue north on US 40 to Granby, then pick up US 34 and drive over rolling sagebrush hills to **Lake Granby,** where a jagged crest of glaciated peaks stands high above the water, extending north into Rocky Mountain National Park. Soon, you'll skirt **Shadow Mountain Lake,** cradled between deeply forested ridges, and pass **Grand Lake,** a lovely dot of water at the mouth of two capacious glacial canyons. The entrance to the park lies just up the road.

Established in 1915, ❻ **Rocky Mountain National Park** ★ ★ *(970-586-1206. Adm. fee)* takes in a magnificent realm of high, broad-backed peaks topped by a vast and dazzling expanse of alpine tundra. Broad glacial canyons gouge the flanks of the mountains, and bare rock walls drop thousands of feet to glimmering alpine lakes. Dense pine forests surround breezy meadows of prairie grass that attract mule deer, elk, bighorn sheep, coyotes, hawks, and owls. Moose wade the mucky wetlands. Eagles soar among the crags. And people cruise over the heights on one of the most spectacular alpine highways in the Rockies—**Trail Ridge Road** ★ ★ *(Closed in winter),* which starts at the park boundary.

At the **Kawuneeche Visitor Center** get an introduction to the park as a whole and learn about the animals and plants that live here on the colder, wetter west side of the park. Then follow the highway up the long, grassy **Kawuneeche Valley,** drained by the infant Colorado River, and look for elk and deer along the forest's edge.

Partway up the valley, stroll through the grounds and buildings of the **Never Summer Ranch** ★, a preserved 1920s dude ranch built by the John Holzwarth family after Prohibition shut down their Denver saloon. Years ago, they charged $11 a week for room, board, and a horse.

Soon, the road switchbacks to **Farview Curve** and a grandstand view of the valley, the meandering course of the Colorado River, and the abrupt wall of the **Never Summer Mountains.** The faint diagonal line cutting across the Never Summers is an irrigation ditch that catches meltwater for farmers near Fort Collins. Farther along, the road reaches **Milner Pass** on the **Continental Divide.** Here, rain falling into tiny **Poudre Lake** eventually flows to the Atlantic, while water rolling off the outhouse roof tumbles toward the Pacific.

Alpine wildflower meadow, Rocky Mountain National Park

Continue your climb above the **Cache la Poudre River** through a subalpine forest that gradually thins, then gives out entirely as you reach the wide, rolling meadows of alpine tundra. Verdant, lush, and bursting with blue, red, and yellow wildflowers during summer, the alpine zone covers roughly a third of the park, opening up heroic vistas of peaks, canyons, and entire mountain ranges.

Drop by the **Alpine Visitor Center** ★ for a primer on how the tiny plants and handful of animals that live here year-round cope with bitter cold, hurricane-force winds, intense sunlight, and often drought-like growing conditions. Also, look for elk in the glacial amphitheater beneath the center's viewing platform.

The road bowls over this incredible landscape for miles, reaching its highest point—12,183 feet—between the **Gore Range** and **Lava Cliffs** turnoffs. Above the parking area at **Rock Cut,** an excellent, self-guiding 1-mile trail loops through tundra meadows.

Next, stop at **Forest Canyon Overlook** ★ and stroll down the path to a viewing platform perched 2,500 feet above the canyon floor. Directly across the abyss, a magnificent rampart of peaks stretches across your field of vision for 20 miles—a grand and ragged wall of gneiss and granite carved by glaciers into bowls and basins, spires, and knife-edged ridges.

The road splits at **Deer Ridge Junction,** but both

View from Longs Peak, Rocky Mountain National Park

## Enos Mills: Park Creator

For the best roadside view of Longs Peak, climb south out of Estes Park on Colo. 7 into the broad Tahosa Valley and pull over at the Enos Mills Cabin. Cowboy, miner, nature guide, and innkeeper, Mills was also a naturalist, author, and the principal lobbyist for the creation of Rocky Mountain National Park, established in 1915. The peak, which Mills climbed repeatedly, rises about 5,200 feet above the floor of the valley and stands directly across from the small homestead cabin he built at age 15. His cabin is open for visits (Mem. Day–Labor Day).

routes lead to Estes Park. To the left, US 34 descends through Horseshoe Park, where bighorn sheep and mule deer often paw the salty soils around **Sheep Lakes.** Straight ahead, US 36 passes the turnoff for Moraine Park, which leads to Rocky's most popular day-hiking destinations—**Bear Lake ★** and **Glacier Gorge ★.**

First homesteaded in 1860 by Joel Estes, his wife, and 14 children, the resort town of **❼ Estes Park** lies in a gently rolling valley surrounded by forested ridges studded with immense domes of granite. High above the rooftops and ridges looms the awesome gray, glacier-gouged peaks that form the scenic heart of Rocky Mountain National Park. Longs Peak, 14,256 feet, stands to the far left.

On the outskirts of town is the sumptuous five-story **Stanley Hotel ★** (*333 Wonderview Ave. 970-586-3371. Tours Mem. Day–Labor Day; rooms, meals available*), built in 1909 by Freelan Stanley, inventor of the Stanley Steamer automobile.

Inspect one of Mr. Stanley's cars, as well as plenty of other memorabilia, at the **Estes Park Area Historical Museum** (*200 4th St. 970-586-6256. Daily May-Sept., Fri.-Sun. Jan.-April; adm. fee*). Next, get a feel for homesteading at the 1870s-era **MacGregor Ranch and Museum ★** (*180 MacGregor Ave. 970-586-3749. June-Aug. Tues.-Fri.*), a 1,200-acre working cattle ranch at the foot of Lumpy Ridge. The

MacGregor family's 1873 home serves as a museum.

For a good view of the town and surrounding area, ride the **Aerial Tramway** *(420 E. Riverside Dr. 970-586-3675. Mid-May–mid-Sept.; adm. fee)* to the top of Prospect Mountain, about 1,400 feet above Estes Park.

From Estes Park, follow US 36 along the base of the mountains to ❽ **Boulder** *(Visitors Bureau, 2440 Pearl St. 303-442-2911 or 800-444-0447)*, an old and enviable university town nestled against the stony foothills

Stanley Hotel, Estes Park

of the Front Range. Gold, silver, and oil once played a part in building up Boulder's Victorian commercial districts and neighborhoods, but today it's a major technical and scientific center where a startling number of people get around on bikes and roller blades.

The city's many nature trails, parks, and greenbelts make the simple act of walking one of the city's greatest lures. On the steep side of town, three major trail systems loop through the **Boulder Mountain Park★**, where you can hike among the great leaning slabs of sedimentary rock called the Flatirons and look down over Boulder and far across the plains. You can also drive to the top of Flagstaff Mountain on the **Flagstaff Mountain Road,** which tops out 1,600 feet above the city.

Boulder's three distinct historic districts include **Chautauqua Park ★** *(900 Baseline Rd. 303-442-3282)*, the only intact Chautauqua site remaining in the West—with its rustic lodge, cottages, and an 1898 auditorium that ranks as a national historic landmark (see sidebar this page).

The **Fiske Planetarium** *(303-492-5002. Call for show times; adm. fee)* on the university campus offers star talks and laser light shows. Then try out the interactive displays at the **National Center for Atmospheric Research** *(1850 Table Mesa Dr. 303-497-1174. Tours)*, where scientists study severe storms and other interesting weather phenomena. The building alone, designed by I. M. Pei, is worth the stop, but so is the setting, high atop Table Mesa, overlooking the plains.

## Boulder's Chautauqua

More than a collection of historical buildings, Boulder's Chautauqua Park still hosts a summer festival of concerts, lectures, silent films, and dance and theater performances. Boulder's program, which started in 1897, was one of thousands modeled after New York's experimental education movement that flowered as the Chautauqua Institution. Today Boulder's Chautauqua is one of only a handful of these enterprises that remain active cultural centers.

**250 miles ● 2-3 days ● Summer through autumn ●
Road between Aspen and Leadville closes in winter.**

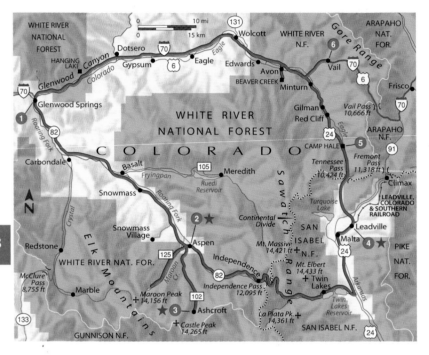

A glorious scenic drive rich in 19th-century mining history, this short but rewarding loop through central Colorado climbs some 6,000 feet over high mountain passes, skirting the state's tallest peaks and some of the world's best known ski resorts. Along the way relax in hot springs and vapor caves, ride an alpine train, and wander ghost towns, museums, and Victorian houses.

From Glenwood Springs, known for its enormous hot springs pool, the route climbs south and east to Aspen, an 1880s silver-mining town turned ski resort and summer arts center. Then it's on to Leadville, a Victorian silver town stuffed with museums, and Vail, another wealthy ski resort with a museum devoted to the sport.

Built at the mouth of a spectacular canyon carved by the Colorado River, **❶ Glenwood Springs** *(Chamber of Commerce, 970-945-6589 or 800-221-0098)* blossomed at the turn of the century as a resort town offering the balmy pleasures of a gigantic hot springs pool and several elegant hotels. Presidents Teddy Roosevelt and Taft may have

soaked here, as did many notable Westerners, including
the tubercular gunslinger and dentist "Doc" Holliday—for
whom the alleged curative waters appear to have done no
great good. He died here at age 35 and is buried in **Lin-
wood Cemetery** *(0.5-mile from Chamber of Commerce).*

The town's magnificent red stone centerpiece, **Hot
Springs Lodge and Pool** ★ ★ *(415 E. 6th St. 970-945-6571.
Adm. fee)* overlooks the Colorado River and bills itself as
the world's largest outdoor natural hot springs pool,
larger than a football field and divided into sections of
varying temperatures. Pull on a swimsuit and step in.

To get really rubber-legged, have a steam bath at **Yam-
pah Spa and Vapor Caves** ★ *(709 E. 6th St. 970-945-0667.
Adm. fee),* a labyrinth of caves and passageways dimly lit
and geothermally heated to 115 pore-dilating degrees.
Above the springs, visit the **Hotel Colorado** ★ *(526 Pine St.
970-945-6511 or 800-544-3998),* a beautifully preserved 1893
hotel whose guest list includes presidents, gangsters, and
pick-and-shovel millionaires from Colorado's mining camps.

East of town, walk, jog, bike, or roller blade along a
16-mile paved path that parallels the Colorado through
**Glenwood Canyon** and intersects with I-70 at four rest
areas. It's a great place to watch white-water boaters, fly
fishers, even rock climbers. At the **Hanging Lake Rest**

Hot Springs Lodge and Pool in Glenwood Springs

**Area ★,** a steep 1.2-mile trail leads to a tiny lake fed by a ring of waterfalls spilling over low cliffs.

From Glenwood Springs, follow Colo. 82 up the Roaring Fork River to ❷ **Aspen ★** *(Resort Assn. 970-925-1940),* built during the 1880s and '90s on a fabulous lode of silver. Originally one of the richest mining towns in the Rockies, Aspen is now one of the region's wealthiest resorts, best known for its skiing, scenery, art galleries, and summer festivals of music, film, food, and wine.

The prosperity of Aspen's mining years is clearly reflected in its Victorian houses and the commercial buildings downtown. These include the 1889 **Hotel Jerome** *(330 E. Main St. 970-920-1000 or 800-331-7213),* a restored luxury hotel built at the height of the silver boom.

To sense how the rich lived, visit the **Wheeler/ Stallard House Museum** *(620 W. Bleeker St. 970-925-3721. Jan.-Easter and mid-June–Sept. Tues.-Fri.; adm. fee),* an 1888 Queen Anne filled with such interesting items as a piano that missionary-physician Albert Schweitzer played during his only trip to this country.

But Aspen's real draw lies outdoors, in the mountains, woods, streams, and meadows that surround the town. To reach the high country quickly, ride the **Silver Queen Gondola ★** *(Base of Aspen Mountain, off Durant St. 970-925-1220, ext. 3598. Mid-June–early Sept., call for winter hours; fare)* to the top of 11,212-foot Aspen Mountain. Here, join up with naturalists from the **Aspen Center for Environmental Studies ★** *(100 Puppy Smith St.*

Preparing to kayak on the Colorado in Glenwood Canyon

*970-925-5756. Mon.-Fri.)* for a free nature hike. The center itself is located in town; phone for a schedule.

The most popular summer outing, by far, follows Maroon Creek up to the **Maroon Bells ★**—14,000-foot peaks, named for their color and shape—rising from the shore of a glacial lake to tower over forests, meadows, and a narrow canyon lined with vermilion mudstone. In summer the road is mostly closed except to buses *(departures from Rubey Park Transit Center; fare).*

For a less crowded excursion, head for ❸ **Ashcroft**

**Ghost Town** ★ *(10 miles S of Aspen on Rte. 102. 970-925-3721. Donations),* an abandoned 1880s mining town built at the base of 14,265-foot Castle Peak.

From Aspen, Colo. 82 threads through spectacular country on its way to 12,095-foot **Independence Pass.**

Aspen trees in autumn, Maroon Bells

Along the way you pass another abandoned mining town, **Independence** *(13.5 miles E of Aspen),* which flared and sputtered during the 1880s. This high road opens up amazing top-of-the-Rockies vistas, but soon narrows to a white-knuckler that snakes down to the headwaters of the Arkansas River. On US 24 north to Leadville, the bulky peaks to your left are 14,433-foot **Mount Elbert,** Colorado's highest summit, and 14,421-foot **Mount Massive,** its second highest.

An 1860s gold camp, then a booming silver-mining center, ❹ **Leadville** ★ and its large Victorian district overlook a forested valley at the foot of Colorado's highest peaks. At 10,430 feet, it's the highest incorporated city in North America. The Chamber of Commerce *(809 Harrison Ave. 719-486-3900)* offers walking tour maps.

In the 1880s Leadville's curious black sand, loaded with silver, helped the fortunes of the Guggenheims and the Dows and built the town into a rowdy, occasionally refined city where Wyatt Earp might tip his hat to Sarah Bernhardt.

On Harrison Avenue, the heart of Leadville's ornate

## Aspen's Silver Boom

By 1890, Aspen had become America's leading silver producer, accounting for a sixth of the nation's output from 1891 to 1893. But the U.S. government's return to the gold standard in 1893 pulled the plug on Aspen and many other silver towns throughout the Rockies. Aspen's resurrection after World War II as a ski resort and summer cultural retreat has given the town a more stable form of prosperity—tourism.

**National Historic Landmark District,** poke into the immaculate 1886 **Delaware Hotel** *(700 Harrison Ave. 719-486-1418 or 800-748-2004),* then wander to the **Western Hardware Co. Museum** *(431 Harrison Ave. 719-486-2213),* an antique shop housed in an 1880s hardware store. Nearby, hoist a few at the 1883 **Silver Dollar Saloon** ★ *(315 Harrison Ave. 719-486-9914),* a dim oasis of carved wood and frosted glass.

Across the street, duck into the 1879 **Tabor Opera House** ★ *(308 Harrison Ave. 719-486-1147. Mem. Day–Labor Day Sun.-Fri.; adm. fee),* built by silver magnate Horace Tabor, Colorado's best known philanderer.

At the far end of Harrison Avenue, get a feel for boarding house life at the 1878 **Healy House** ★ *(912 Harrison Ave. 719-486-0487. Mem. Day–Labor Day; adm. fee),* a Greek Revival stuffed with period articles. Here, too, peer through the windows of the deceptively humble **Dexter Cabin** ★, a tiny log cabin lavishly outfitted as a poker den.

Nearby, visit the **National Mining Hall of Fame and Museum** ★ *(120 W. 9th St. 719-486-1229. Daily May-Oct., Mon.-Fri. Nov.-April; adm. fee),* an ambitious and intelligent interpretation of mining in the United States and, to some extent, the world. Exhibits include mining tools, ore samples, and a few surprises.

On the edge of town is the **Matchless Mine** ★ *(1.5 miles E on E. 7th St. 719-486-0371. June–Labor Day; adm. fee),* where Horace Tabor's second wife, the legendary Baby Doe, died penniless in 1935. Tour her one-room shack, furnished with her meager belongings, and walk through the adjacent hoist building.

Roaring Fork River, Independence Pass

132

For a 2.5-hour train tour of the region, ride the **Leadville, Colorado & Southern Railroad** (*326 E. 7th St. 719-486-3936. Late May–Sept.; fare*) to gorgeous views of 11,318-foot Fremont Pass.

Iron Building, National Historic Landmark District, Leadville

Moving north from Leadville on US 24, descend to the floor of Pando Valley and the ruins of ❺ **Camp Hale,** where alpine troops of the Army's 10th Mountain Division trained for World War II. Most of the 14,000 soldiers who climbed, skied, and trudged through the mountains here took part in a bloody campaign through Italy in the winter of 1944-45.

Continue on US 24 to I-70 east, and take a short side trip to ❻ **Vail** (*Tourism Bureau 970-476-1000 or 800-525-3875*), one of the world's finest and most exclusive ski resorts. Vaguely Tirolean, the town sprang up in the 1960s in a valley between the Gore and Sawatch Ranges. Its shopping district is worth a stroll just for the sticker shock. Skiers will get a kick out of the **Colorado Ski Museum and Ski Hall of Fame** ★ (*Transportation Center, 231 S. Frontage Rd. E. 970-476-1876. Tues.-Sun., closed May and Oct.*), which depicts 120 years of the sport with equipment ranging from homemade Norwegian snowshoes to a pair of Gerald Ford's K2s. There are exhibits on the 10th Mountain Division, ski clothes worn by Olympic racers, and lots of funky old skis.

Along a scenic road in Vail

Glide up to the high country on one of two area ski lifts: in Vail, the **Lionshead Gondola** ★ (*W of central Vail. 970-476-9090. Mid-June–early Sept., call for off-season schedule; fare*); in Beaver Creek, the **Centennial Express Chairlift** ★ (*970-845-9090. Closed May and Oct.; fare*). At the top, join a naturalist for a free guided walk, then hike or mountain bike the trails on your own.

# Along the Gunnison ★

**210 miles ● 2 to 3 days ● Summer and autumn**

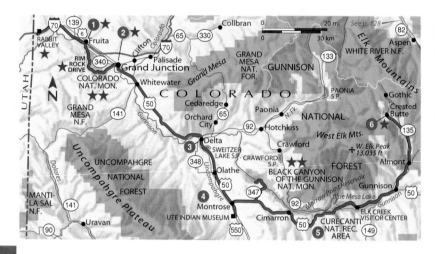

From the desert and mesa country of Grand Junction to the wildflower meadows surrounding Crested Butte, this first-rate scenic trip through west-central Colorado takes in high cliffs of vivid red sandstone, a stunning river chasm, rolling desert hills, and expansive mountain vistas. Along the way, you'll find interesting museums that cover more than the local pioneer scene—dinosaur museums, a re-created fur-trading post, a turn-of-the-century fruit farm, and a collection of vintage mountain bikes.

The route starts with a visit to robotic dinosaurs, then climbs to Colorado National Monument, edging along the eroded brow of an enormous plateau. After stopping in Grand Junction's various museums, it's off to Delta to learn about the fur trade, Montrose for the Ute Indian Museum, and Black Canyon of the Gunnison National Monument. Finally, the route skirts an extensive reservoir of surprising beauty before heading north to the ski and mountain-biking mecca of Crested Butte.

Entering Colorado from Utah on I-70, stop and view dinosaurs in their safely dead form along the self-guiding **Rabbit Valley Trail Through Time** ★ *(Follow signs from I-70 exit 2),* where several skeletons lie exposed and paleontologists dig for bones all summer.

If you have kids aboard, start on the outskirts of **Fruita** at the ❶ **Devils Canyon Science and Learning Center** ★ *(Colo. 340 S. 970-858-7282. Adm. fee),* where dinosaur models roar and swing their great heads from side to side.

Colorado National Monument

Exhibits explore the diet, environment, and differing physical adaptations of herbivores and carnivores, predators and prey. Replicas include several large land and marine reptiles, as well as the younger set's favorite—a Utahraptor that has just ripped the head off a sauropod.

South of Fruita, **Colorado National Monument** ★ ★ *(970-858-3617. Adm. fee)* hugs the abrupt northern edge of the Uncompahgre Plateau and overlooks the Grand Valley of the Colorado River from a height of 1,500 feet. Open, breezy, serene, the park's heart-swelling landscape drops repeatedly into gaping, smooth-walled canyons lined with vermilion-, orange-, and peach-colored stone. Small birds flit among the gnarled branches of juniper and pinyon pine. Colorful lizards zip across the rocks, and desert bighorn sheep turn up from time to time.

From the west entrance, **Rim Rock Drive** ★ climbs through Fruita Canyon amid great broken slabs of stone and balanced rock formations, then edges along the brink of the cliffs for roughly 20 miles before dropping back to the valley floor. The **Visitor Center** provides an overview of the park, and two nearby leisurely hikes explore the pinyon pine forest and traverse the rim of the plateau.

Farther along, gaze across the jumble of red rock towers in **Monument Canyon** ★, then stroll to the tip of the

Dinosaurs at Dinosaur Valley, Grand Junction

**Coke Ovens** ★— 400-foot columns of the same vivid red stone. Pull over at **Highland View** for a great vista across the valley to the **Book Cliffs.** For a quick lesson on how erosion forms the multiple side canyons cutting into the plateau, glance through the interpretive signs at **Upper Ute Canyon, Fallen Rock,** and **Ute Canyon.** Linger at the edge of **Red Canyon**'s ★ 500-foot vermilion cliffs, and pause at **Cold Shivers Point** for one last view from the top before descending to Grand Junction.

An 1880s railroad town and farming center, ❷ **Grand Junction** ★ lies at the confluence of the Gunnison and Colorado Rivers amid extensive irrigated croplands and fruit orchards. Get a feel for old-time farming at **Cross Orchards Historic Site** ★ *(3073 F/Patterson Rd. 970-434-9814. May-Oct. Tues.-Sun.; adm. fee),* an 1896 farmstead with a bunkhouse, packing shed, blacksmith shop, and pens full of animals. Costumed guides show you around and occasionally slap together an apple crate, pound out a horseshoe, or fire up the stove to make treats.

Downtown, the **Museum of Western Colorado** *(248 S. 4th St. 970-242-0971. Mon.-Sat.; adm. fee)* traces the history of the area from the days of the Utes to the present. Its extensive gun collection includes pistols, rifles, and shotguns carried by various outlaws and sheriffs.

Though you'll find some robotics at **Dinosaur Valley** ★ *(362 Main St. 970-243-3466. Daily Mem. Day–Labor Day, Tues.-Sat. Labor Day–Mem. Day; adm. fee),* this large museum focuses more on fossils—their preparation, display, and interpretation. Exhibits identify tooth marks on an immense vertebra and explore comparative anatomy and geology. Children can also excavate and identify dinosaur bones in a mock digging site.

Nearby, kids can mess around with computers, shop in a kid-sized grocery store, and explore many other hands-on exhibits at the **Doo Zoo Children's Museum** ★ (635 *Main St. 970-241-5225. Adm. fee).*

Follow US 50 southeast to ❸ **Delta** and an outstanding living history museum: **Fort Uncompahgre** ★ ★ (205 *Gunnison River Dr. 970-874-8349. Mem. Day–Labor Day Tues.-Sun., March-May Tues.-Sat.; adm. fee).* This crude quadrangle of dirt-roofed cabins and huts re-creates the life of a fur-trading post that operated in this vicinity from 1826 to 1844. Far from casual living history characters, guides here are true buckskinners steeped in the lore—and sometimes the gore—of the fur trade. They trap beaver, hunt with black powder rifles, brain-tan elk and buffalo hides, and hammer out knife blades on an adobe forge. You can participate in some of these activities, or just sit back and listen while your guide explains the history, illustrating his points with traps, strings of beads, tinware, rifles, and other 1830s trade goods.

Farther along US 50 is ❹ **Montrose,** an agricultural supply center and shipping point since the 1880s. Pamphlets describing its modest strip of turn-of-the-century commercial buildings, scattering of lovely Victorian houses, and extensive network of mountain-bike trails are available at the Chamber of Commerce *(1519 E. Main St. 970-249-5515 or 800-873-0244. Mon.-Fri.).*

Browse through rusting farm implements and poke your head into a furnished homesteader's cabin at the **Montrose County Historical Museum** *(Main and Rio Grande. 970-249-2085. Mid-May–Sept. Mon.-Sat.; adm. fee),* housed in the 1912 Denver & Rio Grande Depot.

South of town, the **Ute Indian Museum and Ouray Memorial Park** *(3 miles S on US 550. 970-249-3098. Adm. fee)* displays clothing and other items

MICHAEL LEWIS,
COURTESY COLORADO HISTORICAL SOCIETY

Beaded costume, Ute Indian Museum

that belonged to the Ute chief Ouray and other influential Utes: headdresses, beaded vests and moccasins, pipes, knives, saddlebags, and blankets. Other exhibits trace the history of the tribe and summarize its beliefs. Outside, a self-guiding trail identifies plants and explains how the Utes used them for food and medicine.

A narrow chasm of astounding depth, the **Black Canyon of the Gunnison** cuts across the land as a great

Tomichi Point, Black Canyon of the Gunnison

jagged trench, blackened by shadow and lined with steep walls of dark Precambrian gneiss. **Black Canyon of the Gunnison National Monument** ★★ *(970-249-7036. Adm. fee)* preserves 12 miles of the spectacular gorge, where nearly vertical cliffs plunge more than 2,000 feet from a gently rolling landscape. Mule deer browse shrubs along the rim. Golden eagles and peregrine falcons soar the void, and a constant, static-like hiss rises from the Gunnison River rapids far below.

Get acquainted with the canyon at the **Visitor Center,** then drive along the south rim, where short paths thread among the rocks to knee-tingling overlooks. At Dragon Point gape at the **Painted Wall,** a 2,200-foot cliff rising directly from the river. If you're in good shape and don't mind substituting an 80-foot chain for handholds, you can descend to the river from the Visitor Center and climb back out in a single day *(permit required).*

❺ **Curecanti National Recreation Area** *(970-641-2337)* adjoins Black Canyon of the Gunnison National Monument and stretches east along the river corridor nearly to Gunnison. Here, the land embraces three lakes formed by a series of dams. Two within the canyon, **Crystal** and **Morrow Point,** are long, narrow, and deep. **Blue Mesa Lake,** the biggest in Colorado, floods the relatively open country east of the gorge, runs for 20 miles, and has several narrow arms and many bays. Boat ramps, picnic areas, campgrounds, and nature trails abound, and the lakes are famous for lunker trout.

At **Cimarron** pick up a map of the recreation area and drive through a narrow side chasm into the gorge. Along the way, you'll pass a restored narrow gauge locomotive stranded on a trestle with its tender, freight car, and caboose. Farther east, stretch your legs on the **Dillon Pinnacles** nature trail, and drop by the **Elk Creek Visitor Center** for a primer on the area's human history, which reaches back at least 10,000 years.

An 1870s ranching and mining center along US 50, **Gunnison** *(Chamber of Commerce 970-641-1501)* is now primarily a base for outdoor activities. Two thousand miles of trout streams trickle down from the mountains and meander across the open valley north of town before joining the Gunnison River. It's gold medal trout country, and everybody with a fly rod and a pair of hip boots seems to know it. On summer weekends the more obvious stretches of water can get very crowded.

Follow Colo. 135 north to ➏ **Crested Butte** ★ *(Chamber of Commerce 970-349-6438)*. Site of an 1880s coal-mining town, this thriving ski and mountain biking resort is famed for its wildflowers. Crested Butte was always a steady, modest sort of place, and its false-fronted historical buildings reflect its low-key prosperity.

The real reason for visiting Crested Butte is the spectacular alpine terrain. Hiking and—especially—mountain-biking trails lace the foothills, valleys, meadows, and mountains that rise above town. While many prefer to earn their vertical, the fastest way up is the **Silver Queen Chairlift** ★ at **Crested Butte Mountain Resort** *(970-349-2211. Mem. Day–Labor Day and Nov.-April; fee)*. A second

Biking a Crested Butte byway

chair, the **Keystone** ★, carries mountain bikes as well as passengers to the 12,000-foot summit.

It is befitting that Crested Butte is also home of the **Mountain Bike Hall of Fame and Museum** ★ *(Contact Chamber of Commerce for information)*, a collection of vintage bikes, classic photos, and race memorabilia.

---

### Mountain-Bike Festival

In the summer of 1976, Crested Butte hosted the world's first festival of mountain biking. The Fat Tire Bike Week, an event for everyone from enthusiastic beginners to hardcore racers, traditionally includes guided backcountry tours geared to ability, clinics on mechanics and technique, serious downhill and cross-country races, bicycle polo, bicycle rodeo, "junker jumping," and special programs for kids. Phone the Chamber of Commerce for information.

139

**475 miles ● 4 days ● Summer through autumn**

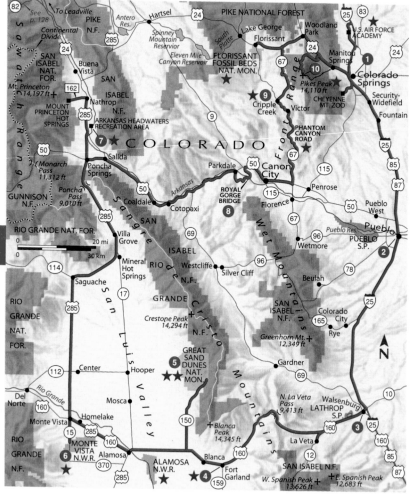

Tremendously varied, this broad loop through central Colorado starts on the Great Plains and follows a ragged crescent of roads through the mountains, valleys, and river chasms southwest of Colorado Springs. Loaded with history, stacked with 14,000-foot peaks, and offering many opportunities to view wildlife, the route takes in forts and mansions, museums, vintage aircraft, immense sand dunes, train rides, fossilized wolf spiders, gambling towns, Olympic athletes, and the Air Force academy.

The route runs south from Colorado Springs to

Walsenberg, then west over the mountains to Monte Vista, with stops at Fort Garland and Great Sand Dunes National Monument. Then it's north for a hot springs dip at Salida, and east along the Arkansas River to spectacular Royal Gorge. A jog to the north takes in the restored Victorian mining town of Cripple Creek, then the

Roping a calf at the Pikes Peak Rodeo, Colorado Springs

loop returns to Colorado Springs by way of Florissant Fossil Beds National Monument and Pikes Peak.

Sprawling across the plains at the foot of Pikes Peak, ❶ **Colorado Springs** *(Visitor Bureau, 104 S. Cascade Ave. 719-635-7506)* was founded as a resort destination in 1871 by railroad tycoon Gen. William Jackson Palmer. Though it has diversified in years since, the city still draws huge summer crowds to its museums, shops, and highly commercialized scenic areas.

Start north of town at the **U.S. Air Force Academy** ★ *(719-472-2555)*, and visit the ultramodern Cadet Chapel, see a planetarium show, stroll around a B-52, and learn about cadet life and Air Force history.

Right across I-25 from the academy's north gate, the **Western Museum of Mining and Industry** ★ *(125 Gleneagle Dr. 719-488-0880. Closed Sun. Dec.-Feb.; adm. fee)* displays colossal steam engines, drills, hoists, and other mining machinery—much of it restored to operating condition.

U.S. Olympic Complex, Colorado Springs

A few miles south, trace the history of rodeo from its frontier roots to its status as a major spectator sport at the **Pro Rodeo Hall of Fame and American Cowboy Museum** ★ *(101 Pro Rodeo Dr. 719-528-4761. Adm. fee)*.

Perhaps the city's best stop is the **U.S. Olympic Complex** ★★ *(1750 E. Boulder St. 719-578-4618. Tours daily)*, where hundreds of Olympic hopefuls train at any given time. As you tour the facilities, you might see gymnasts, boxers, and other athletes honing their skills.

Another fine stop, the **Garden of the Gods** ★ *(1805 N. 30th St. 719-634-6666)* is a tranquil pocket of scrub oak, pinyon pine, and juniper studded with slender towers of smooth salmon-colored stone. It's at its best shortly after sunrise, when the reddish rock glows and tangy, pine-scented air sifts through the hollows. On the park's east side, visit the **Rock Ledge Ranch Historic Site** ★ *(Enter at 30th St. and Gateway Rd. 719-578-6777. June–Labor Day Wed.-Sun., Labor Day–Dec. Sat.-Sun.; adm. fee)*, an excellent living history museum depicting ranch life from 1860 to 1910.

Drive past **The Broadmoor** *(One Lake Ave.)*, a palatial 1918 hotel with 700 rooms, and follow the signs to **Cheyenne Mountain Zoo** *(4250 Cheyenne Mountain Zoo Rd. 719-475-9555. Adm. fee)* and the **Will Rogers Shrine to the Sun** ★—a high stone tower packed with the humorist's memorabilia.

A natural crossroads for hundreds of years, ❷ **Pueblo** *(Chamber of Commerce, 302 N. Santa Fe Ave. 719-542-1704)* grew around the turn of the century from a ranching community famous for its saddlemakers into a major industrial center. Victorian buildings in the **Union Avenue Historic District** include the grand and beautifully restored Union Pacific Depot. But perhaps the best Victorian stop is the lavish 1893 **Rosemount Museum** ★ *(419 W. 14th St. 719-545-5290.*

Spires of stone, Garden of the Gods

*Closed Mon. and Jan.; adm. fee)*, its 37 rooms exceptionally well preserved and decorated with original furnishings.

Reach deeper into the past at the **El Pueblo Museum** *(324 W. 1st St. 719-583-0453. Adm. fee)*, where exhibits span local history from pre-Columbian times to 1900, with special emphasis on the area's native and Latino cultures.

At the **Fred Weisbrod/International B-24 Memorial**

**Museum** ★ *(31001 Magnuson Ave. 719-948-9219)*, wander among more than two dozen vintage military aircraft, look through a Norden bomb sight, and learn about the B-24's role in World War II.

Continue south on I-25 to ❸ **Walsenberg,** then turn west on US 160 to **Lathrop State Park** *(3 miles W on US 160. 719-738-2376. Adm. fee)*, a pleasant spot to unwind among rolling grassland dotted with juniper and pinyon pine, cholla cactus, yucca, and scrub oak. To the south rise the Spanish Peaks; to the west, the Sangre de Cristos. Ducks bob around in the marshy corners of the park's two lakes, while hawks hunt the grasses for rodents and rabbits. Mule deer flick their big ears at passing cars.

Tucked into the foothills beneath the Spanish Peaks, **La Veta** *(Huerfano County Info. 719-738-1065)* grew up around **Fort Francisco** *(Daily Mem. Day–Labor Day, Sat.-Sun. Sept.-Oct.; adm. fee)*, later a trading post. Remnants of the adobe fort—as well as an old saloon, barbershop, and post office—now serve as a local history museum.

About 35 miles west over the Sangre de Cristos stands a more intact frontier outpost, ❹ **Fort Garland Museum** ★ *(Visitor Center, Colo. 159 off US 160. 719-379-3512. Daily April-Sept., Thurs.-Mon. Oct.-March; adm. fee)*. This rectangular cluster of low, sod-roofed adobe buildings was an active Army fort from 1858 to 1883. Soldiers stationed here protected settlers from the Utes and, at Glorietta Pass in 1862, helped turn back Confederate troops from Colorado's gold and silver mines.

Kit Carson commanded the fort during 1866-67. The **Commandant's Quarters,** furnished to resemble Carson's era, contain one of his muzzle-loaded rifles, scabbard, and pocketknife. Most of the other buildings serve as small museums displaying such items as Indian artifacts, ranching implements, wagons, and Latino folk art.

From Fort Garland, take US 160 west and Colo. 150 north to ❺ **Great Sand Dunes National Monument** ★★ *(719-378-2312. Adm. fee)*, an elegant natural dust pan where the tallest sand dunes in North America lie heaped against the foot of the Sangre de Cristo Mountains.

These dunes—about 700 feet high and covering roughly 39 square miles—formed over thousands of years as wind-borne sand swept across the flat San Luis Valley and collected here. The smooth flanks, fulsome mounds, and sinuous crests rest in sensual contrast to the rugged

### Green Chile Sloppers

Looking for a cheap, filling, spicy meal in Pueblo? Then drop by one of the town's taverns and order a green chile slopper, which stacks up from the bottom of the bowl as follows: bun, burger, flood of green chile, pile of shredded cheddar cheese, diced onions, and jalapeños.

Facade along Pueblo's Union Ave.

At the Fred Weisbrod/International B-24 Memorial Museum

mountains cloaked in juniper and pinyon pine.

Drop by the **Visitor Center** for informative exhibits and then roll up your trousers, ford shallow Medano Creek, and amble into the dunes. The climb to the top opens up marvelous views of the dunes and the San Luis Valley, with the Sangre de Cristos to your back, the San Juan Mountains to the west, and the Rio Grande River angling across the valley floor. Perhaps just as rewarding, especially on chilly days: a snooze on the soft, warm sand.

Return to US 160, head west to **Monte Vista,** and take El Rancho Lane 2.5 miles south to the Visitor Center for the ➏ **Alamosa-Monte Vista National Wildlife Refuge Complex** ★ *(938 El Rancho Ln. 719-589-4021).* Pockets of lush wetland areas on the broad desert floor, these refuges harbor thousands of nesting ducks and act as a traditional stopover for the Rocky Mountain greater sandhill crane flock and the handful of endangered whooping cranes that accompany it.

During March, look for the huge sandhills leaping and flapping in elaborate courtship displays. In summer, mountain bluebirds dip over the upland grasses. Snowy egrets and white-faced ibis nest along the sloughs of the Rio Grande, and several types of hawks hunt the wetland meadows. In winter, bald and golden eagles feed here on mallards, gadwalls, pintails, and other waterfowl.

From Monte Vista, follow US 285 to the narrow northern end of the San Luis Valley and climb over Poncha Pass into the Arkansas River Valley. Getting onto this famed white-water and fishing river is easy, thanks to the ➐ **Arkansas Headwaters Recreation Area** ★ *(719-539-7289. Adm. fee),* which stretches roughly 150 miles along the mountain valleys, gorges, and prairie lowlands drained by the Arkansas. Campgrounds, picnic areas, and boat and fishing access sites dot the banks from Leadville to Pueblo.

For a rustic dip, head north to **Mount Princeton Hot Springs Resort** *(County Rd. 162. 719-395-2361),* where natural pools steam beside an icy creek at the base of 14,197-foot Mount Princeton.

**Salida** *(Chamber of Commerce 719-539-2068),* an 1880s railroad town beside the Arkansas, boasts an extensive

144

## Stagecoach Etiquette

The frontier West has always had the reputation for being a wild, often ill-mannered sort of place, but even in the early years attempts were made to enlighten and improve the less refined members of society. One stage line between Pueblo and San Francisco, for example, felt obliged to post the following helpful tips for convivial travel and orderly social discourse: "If you must drink, share the bottle....Spit with the wind, not against it....Don't snore loudly when sleeping."

Hiking in Great Sand Dunes National Monument

historic district of ornate Victorian commercial buildings as well as neighborhoods full of turn-of-the-century houses. Poach your bones at Colorado's largest indoor hot springs, **Salida Hot Springs Pool** *(410 W. Rainbow Blvd. 719-539-6738. Adm. fee),* then follow US 50 east through **Bighorn Sheep Canyon.** Here the Arkansas flows beneath high granite cliffs like a swift sheet of blue-green glass, occasionally shattered by turbulent rapids. Look for bighorn sheep on the steep slopes.

Near Parkdale, take the turnoff for the north entrance of Royal Gorge. Keep an eye out for mule deer as the road curves through rolling grass hills to ❽ **Royal Gorge Bridge** *(719-275-7507. Adm. fee),* spanning a magnificent chasm of pinkish granite 1,250 feet deep. Intensely developed as a gaudy tourist magnet, the place has the air of a theme park. Admission buys a drive across the bridge and rides

Sandhill cranes, Alamosa-Monte Vista National Wildlife Refuge

on an aerial tram, incline railway, and miniature train.

In nearby **Canon City,** step past the gas chamber propped up on the front lawn of the **Colorado Territorial Prison Museum** *(201 N. 1st St. 719-269-3015. Daily May-*

*Aug., Fri.-Sun. Sept.-April; adm. fee).* Inside awaits a tier of cells adorned with billy clubs, cattle prods, and photos of former inmates.

East of Canon City, turn north on Colo. 67, also called **Phantom Canyon Road** ★. A wonderful drive through rough rocky canyons, the road climbs nearly 4,000 feet from the open grasslands around Florence to the sub-alpine forests and views of the high mountains around the restored mining towns of Victor and Cripple Creek.

❾ **Cripple Creek** ★ *(Chamber of Commerce 719-689-2169)* burned to the ground twice before city residents decided that elaborate redbrick Victorian facades might outlast wood. Although today visited by busloads of gamblers who feed the casinos' slot machines and feast on discounted meals, this cheerful, vigorous place, loaded with history, offers much more than games of chance.

Catch a ride through the hills overlooking town on the **Cripple Creek & Victor Narrow Gauge Railroad** ★ *(520 E. Carr St. 719-689-2640. Mem. Day–mid-Oct.; fare).* This weaving, clattering 4-mile journey behind a small coal-fired steam locomotive leads through a ghost town and chugs past mine entrances, tailings piles, and old shaft houses.

While waiting for the next train, browse through pioneer and mining paraphernalia at the **Cripple Creek District Museum** *(511 E. Bennett Ave. 719-689-2634. Daily June-Sept., Sat.-Sun. Oct.-May; adm. fee),* housed in the three-story, brick-and-stone train depot next to the narrow-gauge ticket office.

Riding the rapids of the Arkansas River near Salida

Just north of Cripple Creek, drop 1,000 feet into the **Molly Kathleen Gold Mine** ★ *(719-689-2465. May-Oct.; adm. fee)* to learn how hard-rock miners drill, blast, and haul ore.

Continue north on Colo. 67 to Divide, and then head west on US 24. When you reach Florissant, follow the signs to **Florissant Fossil Beds National Monument** ★ *(Visitor Center 719-748-3253. Adm. fee April-Sept.),* where a wealth of insect and plant fossils lie buried in a classic high-country valley of open prairie grasslands and evergreen forests.

Pikes Peak

Once the site of an ancient lake, the Florissant area was blanketed with mud, pumice, dust, and ash by intermittent volcanic eruptions that started roughly 35 million years ago. Thousands of insects and plants died during the eruptions and settled to the bottom of the lake, where they were preserved as exquisitely detailed fossils. Exhibits at the **Visitor Center** show the shadowlike imprints of various beetles, bees, spiders, and dragonflies—many of them so detailed that their legs, antennae, hair, and wing patterns are visible. You can take a trek along the several nature trails to view the petrified sequoia stumps, then browse through an 1870s homestead, also in the park.

Return to US 24 and follow it east around the base of 14,110-foot ⑩ **Pikes Peak** ★, a grand and bulky mountain that pushes its squat, dome-shaped summit far above treeline. Years ago, one story says, a fellow pushed a peanut to the summit with his nose, but most people prefer to hike, bike, drive 19 miles along the toll road, or board the **Cog Railway** ★ *(719-685-5401. April-Oct.),* which leaves from 515 Ruxton Avenue in Manitou Springs eight times daily in summer, less often in autumn. However you reach the summit, expect tremendous vistas of the Great Plains and the broad back of the Rocky Mountains.

In heavily commercialized **Manitou Springs** *(Chamber of Commerce 719-685-5089),* consider a tour of **Miramont Castle** *(Nine Capitol Hill Ave. 719-685-1011. Closed Mon. Oct.-May; adm. fee)* and its gardens. A sprawling, four-story mishmash of architectural styles, the castle was built at the turn of the century for a French priest and his mother. Some of its rooms have been restored; others contain a doll collection and a miniature model of old Colorado Springs. The price of admission also gains entrance to the railway museum in an adjacent building.

147

**250 miles ● 2 to 3 days ● Summer and fall**

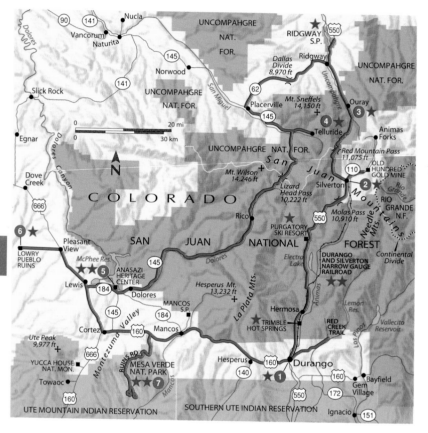

Regarded by some as the state's most spectacular, the San Juan Mountains cut across southwest Colorado as a splintered mass of jagged, glacially mauled peaks and deep canyons streaming with waterfalls. This jaunt takes you through the heart of these mountains, climbing three times to 10,000 feet. It also sails across high desert plains and explores breathtaking river chasms and gorges—some lined with vermilion sandstone. More than a scenic drive, the skyway strings together tidy mining towns, ancestral Puebloan settlements, hot springs, chairlift rides, jeep tours, and a trip on a narrow-gauge steam train.

The drive starts in Durango, departure point for the famous Durango and Silverton Narrow Gauge Railroad, then climbs north to Silverton, Ouray, and Ridgway. From there, it curves around to the resort town of Telluride

and several important Anasazi sites, including the cliff
dwellings at Mesa Verde National Park. Finally, it's back
over the high plains to Durango.

Founded by the Denver & Rio Grande Railway in
1880, ❶ **Durango** ★ *(Chamber of Commerce 970-247-0312)*
was a smelter town where ore from the silver and gold
mines of the San
Juans was
processed and
where vigilantes
shot it out with
outlaws. But
Durango soon
lost its raw edge
as ornate Victo-
rian buildings
sprang up all
over town.

Stroll among
the fine old
houses lining
**The Boulevard**
*(East 3rd Ave.),* a

Scenic vista along US 550 north of Durango

designated historic neighborhood. Then tour the downtown and the 1888 **Strater Hotel** ★ *(699 Main Ave. 970-
247-4431 or 800-247-4431),* a redbrick and gingerbread
extravaganza that still takes guests and dresses its bar-
room staff in period attire.

At the south end of Main stands the 1882 Denver &
Rio Grande train depot, now headquarters for the
**Durango and Silverton Narrow Gauge Railroad** ★★
*(479 Main. 970-247-2733; fee).* Four times a day in summer,
and once a day in winter, a coal-fired steam locomotive
pulls out of the depot trailing a scarf of black smoke and
a line of yellow-and-black 1880s-style passenger cars. The
trains follow the old ore route north, clinging to the precipitous walls of the Animas River Gorge, and arrive in
time for lunch at the 1870s mining town of Silverton. The
scenery is spectacular, the pace civilized, the chuffing
lurch and clickety-clack of the train soothing. Arrange to
spend the night in Silverton, or step off the train midway
for an afternoon (or a week) of hiking or fishing along
the Animas. The 90-mile round trip takes all day.

For a more strenuous excursion from Durango, follow

**Red Creek Trail** *(10 miles NE on E. 3rd Ave., then left at Colvig Silver Camps sign)* 3 miles to the top of Missionary Ridge, which stands 1,600 feet above the Animas River Valley and offers terrific views of La Plata Mountains. However you spend the day, a soak at **Trimble Hot Springs** ★ *(6 miles N on US 550. 970-247-0111. Adm. fee)* is a nice way to cap it off. Or get a grandstand vista in all directions from the chairlift at **Purgatory Ski Resort** ★ *(25 miles N on US 550. 970-247-9000. Late June–Labor Day; adm. fee).*

Heading north, the road climbs from the plateau and canyon country of Durango into the awesome San Juan Mountains. From 10,910-foot Molas Pass, you descend into ❷ **Silverton** ★ *(Chamber of Commerce 970-387-5654 or 800-752-4494).* An old mining town at the foot of stunning 13,000-foot peaks, Silverton retains an air of rustic authenticity despite its crush of gift shops.

In the old days, miners thronged the 40 bars and brothels along Blair Street, while business of a more public nature was conducted in the grand hotels and many shops along Greene Street. Most of the town's old

Red Mountain Creek

buildings survive. Pick up a walking tour pamphlet at the **San Juan County Museum** *(1567 Greene. 970-387-5838. May–Oct.; adm. fee),* housed in the town's 1902 jail and crammed with mining tools, guns, antique kitchenware, and other relics of early Silverton.

To get a hands-on feel for the sort of labor that built the town, take the **Old Hundred Gold Mine Tour** *(5 miles E via Colo. 110. 970-387-5444. Mid-May–mid-Oct.; adm. fee),* which includes a ride on an underground mine train.

Old mining roads crisscross the mountains above Silverton, passing ghost towns, old shaft houses, and an ore bucket tramway. If you don't have four-wheel drive, book a tour through **San Juan Back Country Tours** *(1119 Greene St. 800-4X4-TOUR)* or rent a jeep from one of several local leasing companies. It's also

possible to maneuver many of the roads in a standard
vehicle (with good shock absorbers).

Continue north on US 550 over 11,075-foot Red
Mountain Pass and look for the
dozens of old mine entrances
that pepper the hills. The road
soon curves beneath the aston-
ishing mountains that give the
pass its name—vivid red peaks
with broad smears of red and
orange gravel streaming down
their flanks.

Silverton clock tower

Named for a prominent Ute
chief, ❸ **Ouray** ★ *(Chamber of
Commerce 970-325-4746)* is
another old mining town lined
with splendid Victorian shops and houses. Squeezed
between 14,000-foot peaks and dwarfed by high, multi-
colored cliffs, it lies against the back wall of a narrow
box canyon. On the southwest edge of town, follow the
network of paths, stairways, and suspended boardwalks
into the narrow slot of smooth, purplish limestone
carved by **Box Canyon Falls** ★ *(SW end of town off US 550.
970-325-4746. Adm. fee in summer)*, a thundering jet of
white water that plunges nearly 300 feet.

Breeze through Ouray's historic commercial and residential areas, then drop by the **Ouray County Museum**
*(420 6th Ave. 970-325-4576. Daily May–mid-Oct., call for off-
season hours; adm. fee)*, loaded with photos of old Ouray,
the usual assortment of pioneer appurtenances, and a
couple of homestead cabins out back.

If the rugged heights appeal, look up one of several
outfits running jeep tours into the mountains above
Ouray. Excursions climb to 13,000 feet, visit ghost towns,
and cross the peaks to Telluride, Lake City, and Silverton.

Head underground at the **Bachelor-Syracuse Mine Tour**
*(2 miles E of Ouray on County Rd. 14. 970-325-0220. Mid-May–
mid-Sept.; adm. fee)*, As you ride through the mine, you'll
learn how miners drill and blast shafts, drifts, and stopes.

Finish up with a dip at **Ouray Hot Springs** ★ *(1200
Main St. 970-325-4746. Adm. fee)*, a large outdoor pool with
panoramic vistas of peaks looming 6,000 feet above town.

To the north, above Ridgway, spend a little time at
**Ridgway State Park** ★ *(4 miles N. 970-626-5822. Adm. fee)*,

and enjoy tremendous views of the San Juan Mountains. Self-guiding nature trails and mountain-bike paths loop across rolling grassland hills, through juniper and pinyon woods, and along a reservoir of the Uncompahgre River.

Fall color against winter peaks along the Dallas Divide, west of Ridgway

From Ridgway, head west on Colo. 62, which climbs toward a knockout view of the San Juans' spiny crest at Dallas Divide, then drops to Placerville and the **San Miguel River.** Turn left on Colo. 145 and follow the river up a forested canyon lined with vermilion sandstone to Telluride.

A lovely Victorian mining town founded during the 1870s, ❹ **Telluride** ★ *(Visitor Services 800-525-3455)* lies at the head of a narrow box canyon surrounded by an incredible cirque of 13,000-foot gray rock peaks. Today, it's a booming resort town famous for summer film and music festivals, mountain biking, and ski runs nearly as steep as the price of its real estate.

Most of the finer buildings of the **historic district** ★ were built after the Rio Grande Southern Railway laid track to the town in 1890. They include the railroad's 1891 depot, now a microbrewery; the 1895 miners' hospital, now the **Telluride Historical Museum** *(Gregory and N. Fir Sts. 970-728-3344. Call for hours; adm. fee);* and the 1891 **New Sheridan Hotel** ★ *(231 W. Colorado Ave. 970-728-4351)*, which is still happily accepting guests.

Poke around downtown, then hike or mountain bike to the brink of **Bridal Veil Falls** ★, a long ribbon of foam spilling 365 feet from the cliffs behind town. Trails to the falls also lead to a high glacial basin carpeted with wild-flowers. If you'd rather not walk, several operators run jeep tours into other high-country areas where you can visit mining ruins and ghost towns.

From Telluride, follow Colo. 145 south past the mouths of capacious glacial canyons lined with 13,000-foot peaks. The highway tops out at 10,222-foot **Lizard Head Pass,** then follows the **Dolores River** down through colorful layers of sedimentary rock to the mesas and high desert plains of southwest Colorado—an area dotted with thousands of dwellings that once belonged to the ancestors of modern Pueblo Indians.

West of Dolores, get a terrific introduction to these ancient Pueblo peoples at the ❺ **Anasazi Heritage Center** ★ ★ *(2 miles W on Colo. 184. 970-882-4811).* The name they are known by, Anasazi, is not Pueblo but Navajo; it means "ancient enemies." The innovative museum depicts the evolution of the northern San Juan culture from A.D. 1 through A.D. 1300. Artifacts illustrate the life of these people from the early years of hunting with an *atlatl* (a spear-throwing device) through the development of highly efficient dry farming techniques, permanent settlements, and far-flung trade routes.

Pick up a self-guiding brochure and step outside for a look at **Dominguez Ruin,** circa 1120, a small, four-room dwelling. At the top of the hill, you'll find the more extensive **Escalante Ruin** ★, which offers panoramic views of the region.

Northwest of Dolores, the ❻ **Lowry Pueblo Ruins** ★ *(W on Colo. 184, N on US 666, W 9 miles from Pleas-ant View. 970-247-4082. Check on driving conditions)* stand on a gentle rise overlooking Sleeping Ute Mountain. Once home to about a hundred people who hunted small game and raised corn, beans, squash, and tobacco, this dwelling was started about A.D. 1060 and eventually expanded into a large three-story, 40-room pueblo with eight kivas, or circular ceremonial chambers, including one of the largest great kivas in the region. A self-guiding tour leads you through the ruins.

153

Inside the Fifth Kiva, Mesa Verde N.P.

In a spectacular setting overlooking the plateaus, canyons, and valleys of the Four Corners region, **7 Mesa Verde National Park ★ ★** *(970-529-4465. Adm. fee; very crowded in July-August)* preserves the cliff dwellings and villages built by the Anasazi between A.D. 550 and 1270. Drawn, perhaps, by the high mesa's moist climate, timber, and abundant game, they first settled in small clusters of pit houses, then built upright pole-and-adobe structures, and eventually erected compact villages of double-coursed stone walls rising two or three stories.

All of these types of settlements were built on top of the mesa, among fields of corn, squash, and beans. Not until around A.D. 1200 did these peoples—for unknown reasons—begin building their famous cliff dwellings. And then, within a hundred years, and perhaps because of drought and an intensifying shortage of

Moonrise over the San Juan Mountains, above Ridgway

natural resources, they appear to have deserted them.

It's a pleasantly eerie sort of place, cryptic, beautiful, sacred for some, and made all the more puzzling for everyone because, even after a hundred years or so of anthropological research, we are still learning about the people who lived here.

Follow the long winding road along the mesa's north rim to the **Far View Visitor Center** ★, take time to admire the incredible vista, and pick up tickets *(fee)* for a ranger-led tour of **Cliff Palace** ★ ★ or **Balcony House.** Then drive out to **Chapin Mesa** and go through the park's **museum** ★ before clambering down to the sandstone dwellings with your group. Afterward, take some time to idle on the **Ruins Road** ★, which hugs the rims of side canyons and offers views of many cliff dwellings, as well as mesa-top pit houses and pueblos.

**U.S. FOREST SERVICE campground reservations for Montana, Idaho, Wyoming, and Colorado 800-280-2267**

### MONTANA

*Travel Montana* 406-444-2654 or 800-847-4868. General information.
*Department of Transportation* road and weather conditions 800-332-6171.
*Department of Fish, Wildlife and (State) Parks.* Information 406-444-2535. Hunting and fishing licenses 406-329-3511.
*Glacier National Park.* Information 406-888-5441. Campground reservations 800-365-2267.

### IDAHO

*Idaho Tourism* 800-847-4843 or 800-VISIT-ID. Information on outfitters, guides, camping, outdoor recreation, ski conditions, and maps.
*Department of Transportation* road conditions 208-336-6600.
*Idaho Non-Resident License Buyer Program* 800-554-8685. Fishing and hunting licenses.
*Idaho Outfitters and Guides Assoc.* 208-342-1919. Has list of seasonal guides and outfitters.

### WYOMING

*Wyoming Tourist Office* 307-777-7777 or 800-225-5996. General vacation information.
*Department of Transportation* travel conditions 307-635-9966.
*Grand Teton National Park* 307-739-3600. General information.
*Wyoming Game and Fish Department.* Wildflowers guide, birds brochure, hunting and fishing information 307-777-4600. Nonresident hunting and fishing licenses 307-777-4597.
*Yellowstone National Park.* Information 307-344-7381. Campground reservations 307-344-7311.

### COLORADO

*Colorado Travel and Tourism Authority* 800-265-6723. General travel information and hotel and motel reservations.
*Department of Transportation* road conditions 303-639-1234.
*Colorado Division of Wildlife* 303-291-7299. Information on hunting and fishing seasons, conditions, fish stocking locations, camping.
*Mesa Verde National Park* 970-529-4465. General information.
*Rocky Mountain National Park* Information 970-586-1206. Campground reservations 800-365-2267.
*State campground* reservations 800-678-2267.
*State Office of Outfitter Registration* 303-894-7778. Has list of seasonal guides and outfitters.

### HOTEL & MOTEL CHAINS
*(Accommodations in all four states unless otherwise noted)*

Best Western International 800-528-1234
Budget Host 800-BUD HOST (Except Idaho)
Choice Hotels 800-4-CHOICE
Clarion Hotels 800-CLARION (Except Wyo.)
Comfort Inns 800-228-5150
Days Inn 800-325-2525
Doubletree Hotels and Guest Suites 800-222-TREE (Colo., Idaho only)
Econo Lodge 800-446-6900
Embassy Suites 800-362-2779 (Except Mont.)
Fairfield Inn by Marriott 800-228-2800
Friendship Inns Hotel 800-453-4511
Hampton Inn 800-HAMPTON
Hilton Hotels 800-HILTONS (Colo.,Wyo. only)
Holiday Inns 800-Holiday
Howard Johnson 800-654-2000
Independent Motels of America 800-841-0255
La Quinta Motor Inns, Inc. 800-531-5900 (Colo., Wyo. only)
LRI Loews Hotels 800-223-0888 (Except Mont.)
Motel 6 800-466-8356
Quality Inns-Hotels-Suites 800-228-5151
Radisson Hotels Intl. 800-333-3333 (Colo., Mont. only)
Ramada Inns 800-2-RAMADA
Red Lion 800-547-8010
Red Roof Inns 800-843-7663 (Except Mont.)
Ritz-Carlton 800-241-3333 (Colo. only)
Sheraton Hotels & Inns 800-325-3535
Super 8 Motels 800-843-1991
Travelodge International, Inc. 800-255-3050. (Except Wyo.)
Westin Hotels and Resorts 800-228-3000 (Colo. only)
Wyndham Hotels and Resorts 800-822-4200 (Colo. only)

### NOTES ON AUTHOR AND PHOTOGRAPHER

THOMAS SCHMIDT has written extensively about the nature and history of the Rocky Mountain region. His work includes books on Glacier, Rocky Mountain, and Grand Teton National Parks, as well as on Wyoming history. He has contributed to several previous National Geographic books and is co-author of *The Northern Rockies* in the Smithsonian Guides to Natural America series. Schmidt lives in Idaho, among the western foothills of the Teton Range, with his wife, Terese, and son, Patrick.

Photographer MICHAEL LEWIS has been living in Colorado since 1986. His first book, *Colorado's Centennial Farms and Ranches,* told the stories of some of Colorado's original settlers. Lewis lives in Denver with his wife, Sharon, and their two dogs, Carlos and Lucy. He visited Idaho and Montana for the first time for this book, his first for the Society.

# *Index*

**157**

160

Composition for this book by the National Geographic Society Book Division. Printed and bound by R.R. Donnelly & Sons, Willard, Ohio. Color separations by Digital Color Image, Pensauken, New Jersey. Paper by Consolidated/Alling & Cory, WillowGrove, Pennsylvania. Cover printed by Miken Companies, Inc. Cheektowaga, New York.

Library of Congress Cataloging-in-Publication Data

Schmidt, Thomas, 1959-
    National Geographic's driving guides to America.   The Rockies / by Thomas Schmidt ; photographed by Michael Lewis ; prepared by the Book Division, National Geographic Society.
        p.    cm.
    Includes bibliographical references and index.
    ISBN 0-7922-3423-5
    1. Rocky Mountains Region — Tours. 2. Automobile travel — Rocky Mountains Region—Guidebooks.   I. Lewis, Michael, 1952 Feb. 5-   II.   National Geographic Society   (U.S.).   Book Division.   III. Title.
F721.S345   1996
   917.804'33—dc20                          96-7740
                                                  CIP